He Leads Me Beside Still Waters

50 Love Letters of Healing and Restoration from our Lord

Steve Porter

He Leads Me Beside Still Waters

Copyright © 2015 Steve Porter

ISBN-13: 978-1501028038

All Rights Reserved. No part of this publication may be reproduced, stored in a retrieval system or transmitted in any form or by any means – online, electronic, mechanical, photocopy, recording or any other – except for brief quotations in printed reviews, without prior permission of the author.

All Scripture quotations, unless otherwise specified, are from the King James Version of the Bible (Copyright © 1977, 1984, Thomas Nelson Inc., Publishers.)

This book is dedicated to the glory and adoration of God and to all who desire a closer walk with Him.

"There is hope even if a tree has been cut down that at the scent of water it will sprout again ."

(Job 14: 7-9)

Pay no attention to the howling of the wind, or voices in your ear
God will make a way through the wilderness and hold you close and near.

While you think He's rather distant and forgotten you all the same
That is when He's close to you and calling you by name.

He is holding your hand when you think He is all but gone
He is weeping understanding tears with you when feel you don't belong.

On the other side of the wilderness is a feast prepared for you,
a promised land given through intervention that is true.

Now comes that special garden of roses that was spoken,
in abundance now you grow and flourish like an ocean.

His promise now fulfilled has made you stronger still,
thanks to the wilderness where you crucified your will.

Acknowledgements

Special thanks to our editors and publishing team, Nancy Arant Smith, Matt Rowland, Ken Darrow, M.A.

Special thanks most of all to our Beloved Daddy God, who holds us so close in the palm of His hand.

TABLE OF CONTENTS

Acknowledgements v
Preface ix
Introduction 1
The Long Journey Home 3
Trust Me 5
Fix your Gaze on Me 8
Those Walls Must Come Down 10
Disappointment 13
Strengthening of Heart 16
Quickening Presence 19
Unconditional Love 21
My Glorious Presence 24
Purity of Mind 26
Never Give Up or Give in 29
Getting to the Root 31
Freedom 35
The Ointment that Soothes all Pain 38
Be Careful What Grabs Your Heart 40
Controlling Your Thought Life 42
Contending 46
Little Foxes that Spoil the Vine 50
Oaks of Righteousness 54
He Leads Me Beside the Still Waters 56
My Brooding Presence 58
Eye of the Dove 60

Ask. Seek. Knock.	63
Holy Desperation	66
Beholding and Becoming	69
Praying and Singing the Scriptures	73
Eternal Weight of Glory	76
The Threshing Floor	82
Honey in the Carcass	85
Your Identity is Found in Me	88
In the Wilderness	91
Finding Rest in the Wilderness	94
Apple of My Eye	97
I Never Sleep	100
Can I Call You Friend?	103
Come Away with Me	105
Running After Me	108
Keeping Me Company	110
Seasons of Life	112
Yet... I will Rejoice	116
Savor What Really Matters	120
Let Your Light so Shine	123
The God of the Turn Around	126
In Remembrance	129
Unknowns	131
Those That Have Been Forgiven Much Love Much.	133
My Recovery Room	136
Unknotting of Knots	141
I Will Restore You	145
Let My Kingdom Come!	148

Preface

I do not believe that my writing is sacred or that I hold new revelations, nor am I writing a new version of Scripture. The Bible is, of course, the only inerrant Word of God; our writings must be consistent with that unchanging standard. Many within the church today believe that the prophetic movement is still at work. We also believe that the Holy Spirit speaks to all in a still small voice, but all that we share through reading Scripture and prayer, and through time with the Holy Spirit, must be backed up with scripture. The Holy Spirit is our teacher and He takes the things that are Jesus' and reveals them to us. He talked to OT people; He gave David songs, prophets warnings, Apostles instructions and commands and wisdom. I believe there is enormous value in learning to wait quietly in God's Presence, but all prophetic impressions and messages must be Word centered. I would also conclude that the main devotional source should be Scripture. Within these pages are the words and Scriptures Jesus lovingly laid on my heart. May they bring comfort and encouragement to you as well. This is a unique prophetic devotional book and wonderful aid that can be used alongside the Scriptures in daily quiet time with the Lord.

Introduction

The enemy who entraps the vulnerable will be pushed back, as the Lord has a loving message to comfort those taken hostage or left wounded on the spiritual battlefield: **"I will never give up on you, no matter how desperate your need. I am here for you, with a plan to raise you up."**

He Leads Me Beside Still Waters was created to bring encouragement, conviction, hope, and comfort. You are so very special to God, you are always on His heart. Our Lord desires to speak a loving message of healing and restoration into your life. Come and meet with your Beloved Savior—you will find Jesus in the pages of this prophetic devotional.

I encourage you to read this book carefully and prayerfully, bit by bit, searching always for the word of the Lord for your own personal needs.

Come close to the Lord and sit with Him awhile for you are sweet and beautiful to His heart. His voice is soothing; His countenance is lovely; beautiful are His words to you. They refresh your soul and call you deeper into His presence. Oh, the depths of His love for you!

Steve Porter

He delights to draw close to His bride. His eyes are always on all their troubles, but His wounded warriors shall flourish once more—brighter, more sweet, more lovely, more beautiful, more glorious, purer, more shining, more fair! They shall carry the glorious presence of their Lord—and shall flourish forever in the courts of our God! As you prayerfully read *He Leads Me Beside Still Waters* may you be cultivated, watered, tended, moved, pruned, and trained by the Lord Jesus Himself.

Read on.

The Long Journey Home

"He lets me rest in green meadows; he leads me beside peaceful streams. He renews my strength. He guides me along right paths, bringing honor to his name. Even when I walk through the dark valley of death, I will not be afraid, for you are close besides me. Your rod and your staff protect and comfort me." (Psalms 23:2-4)

My Precious Child,

I know the journey has been hard. You have become weary and tired in the battle. Sometimes you even question where I am and whether or not I love you. I want you to know I am here always, even to the ends of the earth.

When you feel lost and can no longer see clearly ahead—when the darkness of the night wipes out your sight—when you feel that your choices have led you to a place of aimless wandering, know this: I will lead you out.

Imagine a child who is lost in a dense, dark forest at night with no light or sense of direction. He's terrified that he may be devoured by the darkness or, worse yet, by the wild creatures of the night. Yet out of the darkness comes a beacon of hope—someone to pick him up and rush him back to the safety of his parents' arms.

I am that beacon of HOPE for you. No matter how you lost your way or how deep your level of panic, I will come and rescue you. Together we'll begin the long journey out of the forest of confusion and affliction, out of the forest of poor choices to a place of restoration, stability and victory.

Can you see Me standing there with a lantern in My hand ready to guide you out? I will be that light to your path and lamp to your feet. I am your light! I am your beacon of hope! Put your hand in Mine, and let me guide you to rest with me awhile beside gentle streams, at the edge of lush, green meadows where my abiding presence flows. I will guide you out of the valley of death into the protective shelter of My love. I am your refuge and strength—and as you hide yourself in Me, My Spirit will bring you to a place of comfort and rest.

No one is so terribly lost that I, the Lord, cannot lead them out of the darkness into the light. No one is too far gone that I cannot rescue them. I see where you are even now and am gently pulling you into my arms. So call upon Me, for I will never fail to answer your call. You are Mine, and I will never let you go.

Trust Me

«Some trust in chariots, and some in horses: but we will remember the name of the LORD our God.»
(Psalms 20:7)

"O LORD of hosts, blessed is the man that trusts in you."
(Psalms 84:12)

My Precious Child,

When everything seems to be going wrong, when you face drought and difficulties, trust Me.

Take joy in the God of your salvation,

Find your joy and peace in Me alone,

Not in what I do or don›t do,

What I permit or do not, for I am still the same God regardless of how things go.

Even when you don′t understand—

I am your strength, so derive your faith from who I Am,

Because I never change,

Nor does My love wane, even when you don′t understand.

Walk the walk of faith, not based on what you see with your natural eyes, but on who I Am. Do you want to find peace, even in your unanswered questions? Then focus on My face, My love and My faithfulness as well as your identity in Me. For you are like hinds′ feet on high places, secure and never shaken as long as you are in Me.

Put your faith in My character in spite of what I do or don′t do. Don′t look with your natural eyes, but look with heaven′s eyes, the eyes of faith and fall in love with Me all over again...

It is written, My tender child:

> **"Trust God from the bottom of your heart;**
>
> **don't try to figure out everything on your own.**
>
> **Listen for God's voice in everything you do, everywhere you go;**
>
> **he's the one who will keep you on track.**
>
> **Don't assume that you know it all.**

He Leads Me Beside Still Waters

Run to God! Run from evil!
Your body will glow with health,
your very bones will vibrate with life!
Honor God with everything you own;
give him the first and the best.
Your barns will burst,
your wine vats will brim over.
But don't, dear friend, resent God's discipline;
don't sulk under his loving correction.
It's the child he loves that God corrects;
a father's delight is behind all this."

(Proverbs 3:5-12, MSG)

Fix your Gaze on Me

"Fixing our eyes on Jesus, the pioneer and perfecter of faith..."
(Hebrews 12:2)

My Precious Child,

Do you not know that I love you with a love so deep that mere words cannot adequately describe it? Do you know that you are always in my heart? I see that you're carrying an incredibly heavy burden. I know this burden well for I carried one myself when I walked the earth. I am not so far removed from your life that I do not understand. I do know and I do care for you.

I want you to see that I am here. I am holding you close to me even now. I want to hear what you have to say—every concern, every burden. Cast all your cares on me for I care for you, my child. You do not have to carry your burdens alone. I say once more—I am here. I will catch you when you fall. I will hold you close and never let go.

I am all you need. I am what you long for, deep in your

soul, and I am here to draw you unto myself. I am wooing you into intimacy—to take you deeper in my presence. Unload your burdens and sit with me awhile.

I miss my time with you. You have been so preoccupied with your trials that you seldom come to me for sweet fellowship anymore. Your burdens have caused worry and fear, but my perfect love for you will cast out fear and worry. Do not allow these things to steal you away from my presence. Do not hide away alone, tormented by your struggles.

Your mind strays away from me and fixates on the burdens you carry, distracted by the things around you. Instead fix your gaze on me for I am all you need. Hide in my presence and dump those worries at my feet, for I will see you through!

I want you to become conscious of me and my abiding presence, so you will see that I do care and that I will answer you. The enemy is lying to you, trying his best to convince you that I have forgotten you and that I don't care. But where can you go to escape my loving embrace and tender compassion? There is no place you can go where I am not with you. I will hold you close to my heart forever, for you are mine and I treasure you. Did I not say in Proverbs 4:25: **'Let your eyes look straight ahead; fix your gaze directly before you,'** for I am standing there with open arms? I cherish you, so look and behold me. Come, let us spend time together, my beloved, so I can refresh and encourage you.

Those Walls Must Come Down

"When the people heard the sound of the rams' horns, they shouted as loud as they could. Suddenly, the walls of Jericho collapsed, and the Israelites charged straight into the town and captured it."
(Joshua 6:20, NLT)

My Precious Child,

Oh how I long to take you gently by the hand and lead you to My banqueting table. I've already set a place for you there, and I'm bidding you to come and feast on My presence and be changed. For I have removed the veil and given you free access to My heart.

Come and bring nothing but yourself, for we have an appointment that will change your life. You will enter a new place in Me where strongholds will be cut away, and old ways of doing things will be altered. Today is a day of freedom where you can walk out of the prison house into My banqueting house where My banner over you is love.

Even as the walls of Jericho came tumbling down, I long

to see the walls that separate us be torn down. My perfect love will cast down every evil thing that enslaves you, and, as you surrender your life totally to Me, I will lead you out of bondage and into a special place where we can share a closeness found nowhere else. Realize that Satan has come to torment you, convincing you that you'll never be free, but I will have the final word! Those walls must come down.

In that special place you'll be given revelation not found in books. I will reveal Myself to you in such a powerful way that even the greatest strongholds will fall away. You will see and grasp My heart cry more clearly than ever before, and take great delight in being on the Lord's side. As you bask in My presence I will strengthen and empower you to win over the enemy. In fact, you will put him to flight effortlessly, using My name and your authority.

I'm calling you to begin to praise Me, especially when you can't see through the darkness ahead, for even the darkest night cannot hide My face from you when your lips choose to praise Me. Remember that I always sent the praise team first when the Children of Israel went to battle, and walls fell before them without raising a sword.

My ears are tuned to My children who cry out for freedom. I will never turn away a truly repentant heart. In fact, I will come and rescue them and tear down their prison walls. I will give them a new battle song that will burst forth with praise, to shake the kingdom of darkness and consecrate the ground on which they walk.

I'm tearing down the walls that hold you captive, and as you praise Me you will see My face. Brick by brick I'm breaking through before you, as you submit and give Me first place.

Answer this question: What kind of walls stand between us, hindering you from going deeper with Me? Whether you see them or not, those walls hinder your walk with Me. So ask Me to shatter those walls, so that nothing comes between us again.

You are My treasure. And although I love you, I can only take great delight in you when you're fully yielded to Me. In fact, I will not take a back seat to anything in your life. As things get harder and days get darker, you will not outwit the enemy unless you are on the Lord's side. So which way will you go? Get off the fence, and be victorious. The choice is yours...

Disappointment

"But Jesus said unto him, No man, having put his hand to the plow, and looking back, is fit for the kingdom of God."
(Luke 9:62)

My Precious Child,

The path to maturity is paved with intense effort, and though I will ultimately lead you through to great victory, you will face disappointments along the way.

This path is also known as the high road of surrender, because it's only as you yield and surrender your disappointments to My sovereignty that I can use them for My glory.

Here's the secret: Glean the hidden treasure from every disappointment. You'll always discover gold within every trial if you're willing to search for it. The thing is that most never bother to look below the surface to find the incredible treasures hidden there. This hidden treasure is an inner wealth, a richness of spirit and special revelation of who I am.

When you encounter disappointment along the road, the enemy will also try to convince you that all is lost. However, the truth is that you gain much in the spiritual realm, growing in stature while increasing in wisdom and anointing. The devil, who is a liar, wants you to lose hope, believing the issue will never be resolved, and that it is over forever. He makes it appear that the problems are too great for Me to address. Those doubts drain your spirit and hinder your progress toward maturity. He also wants you to forsake your divine purpose and destiny by letting go of your vision.

My child, disappointment is an inevitable fact of life. As you're alive, there will be highs and lows, ups and downs, laughter and weeping, happiness and sadness. Life can sometimes feel like a perilous roller coaster ride. Many struggle with feelings of despair when things go wrong. When dreams are shattered and hope dies, disappointment is the natural result. Pain is inevitable. Why? Because you live in a fallen world.

But I don't want that to hinder you in any way. In order for you to have everything I want to give you, you'll have to let go of bitterness and dump every heavy weight at My feet so I can set you free and heal your disappointment. However, that will never happen until you let go of your right to be angry. I can turn every dark thing around for your good if you dump it in My lap.

My still, small voice will comfort you through my Word:

'Don't be afraid, for I am with you. Don't be discouraged,

for I am your God. I will strengthen you and help you. I will hold you up with my victorious right hand.' (Isaiah 41:10)

I will be your strength, your hope, your comfort and your Counselor. In times of weakness I will be faithful to meet your needs and lift you above your circumstances. Trust Me to be everything you need, for I am always more than enough!

Pray this bold prayer right now!

"I will lift up my eyes to the hills— From whence comes my help?

My help comes from the Lord, Who made heaven and earth.

He will not allow your foot to be moved; He who keeps you will not slumber.

Behold, He who keeps Israel shall neither slumber nor sleep.

The Lord is your keeper; The Lord is your shade at your right hand.

The sun shall not strike you by day, Nor the moon by night.

The Lord shall preserve you from all evil; He shall preserve your soul." (Psalms 121 : 1-8)

Strengthening of Heart

"Wait on the LORD: be of good courage, and he shall strengthen thine heart: wait, I say, on the LORD."
(Psalms 27:14)

My Precious Child,

Calamity of Heart, you cry! "All is lost and my heart is weak and broken. If you could peel the skin back to expose everything underneath, the world would plainly see the damage afflicting my soul."

Right now My word to you is alive and powerful if you will respond to it. It is sharper than the sharpest two-edged sword, cutting between soul and spirit, between joint and marrow. **This word has quickening power—you are to "Wait on Me…"**

Yes, wait on Me. Hold your wounded heart out to Me and I will strengthen you. As you hold still and allow my Spirit to calm your fears and worries I will pour over you healing oil. Be of good courage, for I am gracious, slow to anger and abounding in love. I will show myself faithful and powerful in mending your heart—only come and wait on Me to touch you. **'Be still and know that I am God!'** (Psalms 46:10)

Do not rush this process. Let rivers of living water flow over the scarred places of your heart, until I fill your heart with My tender love that heals and restores as nothing else can.

When I begin to blow My healing breath upon your heart you will feel like you are coming alive and will be tempted to run back out to the battlefield prematurely. Hold steady and refuse to budge from that secret place of waiting until I give you the signal. Then you will be a mighty warrior—ready, eager and empowered to win!

As you wait and hold still I will do a deep work in you. Like a skilled surgeon who cuts away the infected parts, I will cut away all anger, bitterness, resentment, and carnal works of the flesh. I will remove every harmful thing from within your soul while cleansing you with healing waters.

'And I will give you a new heart, and I will put a new spirit in you. I will take out your stony, stubborn heart and give you a tender, responsive heart' so you more closely reflect the heart of your Heavenly Daddy. (Ezekiel 36:26)

The healing process is critical, so let me stress again, do not rush Me. Only wait and watch your Great Physician and Healer restore you to perfect health. You will become my masterpiece! I am not through with you, so stay put, and patiently wait for My healing water to saturate and restore you. My water will purify you and set you apart for Myself, giving you a heart of flesh for a heart of stone, so you can work in unity with Me, and together we can change the world!

Quickening Presence

"It is the Spirit Who gives life [He is the Life-giver]; the flesh conveys no benefit whatever [there is no profit in it]. The words (truths) that I have been speaking to you are spirit and life."
(John 6:63, AMP)

My Precious Child,

Don't you know how much I want to quicken your spirit with My power? I know you feel weak and are tempted to give up. But don't throw in the towel because, if you let me, I will touch you deep in your spirit and awaken you again. I am the **Life-giver,** and I have the power to make you live again.

You can no longer feel that life-giving power flowing through you, because you've become increasingly weak from the fight. You feel like a field of burned grass that has been far too long without water. But take heart, because I will breathe on you and awaken your spirit with My mighty power, quickening you so you will once again resemble lush and fertile green grass.

I will impart truth to you—a divine revelation of me—for even as a flower unfolds its petals so will My quickening words unfold truth to you and you will flourish. I am the life-giver.

I am drawing you unto myself even as I said in my Word in

John 12:32-33, NKJV: **"And I, if I am lifted up from the earth, *will draw all peoples to Myself."***

I will awaken your heart and soul as you give Me full control of your life. I will breathe into your spirit a new sense of desperation and hunger for no one and nothing but Me. Cry out to Me, My child, and I will open your eyes so you can see Me dwelling in you ... so that you can sense My life-changing presence.

I will inspire you, making you come alive. I will invigorate and stir you. I will transform you and stimulate you to greater faith. I will energize you and excite you in My quickening presence!

I am awakening you to discern new realms of my spirit, pouring out my glory on you afresh. Just as you sit in a sunny window to let the sun warm you when you're cold, so my spirit will warm and comfort you with my life-giving presence. You will bask in my glory, as spirit and life begin to fill, heal and restore you, and you will never be the same again, because all things have suddenly become new!

Unconditional Love

"I led them with cords of human kindness, with ties of love. To them I was like one who lifts a little child to the cheek, and I bent down to feed them."
(Hosea 11:4, NIV)

My Precious Child,

My heart goes out to you, knowing you feel inadequate and insecure. You fear that I will turn you away because you have let Me down. You carry deep wounds from past failures that the devil won't let you forget. But hear Me when I say I love you unconditionally, no matter what. So now is the time to put away insecurity and believe Me when I say you are Mine and I will never let you go. Believe My Word when it says, **'No good thing does He withhold from those who walk uprightly.'** (Ps. 84:11) Believe Me when I say, **'Whatever you ask in My name without doubting, you shall have it.'** (John 14:12) When I say, **'Call upon Me, and I will answer you and show you great and mighty things.'** (Jer. 33:3) When I say, **'Nothing can separate you from the love of God, not even peril or sword.'** (Rom. 8:35) When I say, **'Behold, I**

have given you power to tread on serpents and scorpions… and nothing shall by any means harm you.' (Luke 10:19) When I say, **'By His stripes you are healed.'** (Isa. 53:5) When I say, **'Even in old age they will still produce fruit; they will remain luxuriant and green.'** (Ps. 19:14) How many ways must I say it before you grab hold of it and choose to believe without doubting?

Your identity is secure, so rise up and see yourself through Heaven's eyes—a mighty warrior who never needs to be afraid or ashamed. So run to Me, run into My open arms with whatever ails you, knowing that I have already anticipated your need and have made a way of escape for you. And not only that but I have crowned you with glory and honor—I have set before you a destiny you can't even imagine, if you will only live as if you believe My Word.

Jeremiah 31:3 Long ago the Lord said to Israel: **'I have loved you, my people with an everlasting love. With unfailing love I have drawn you to myself.'**

No one can change this fact; My love for you never changes. I have freed you from bondage and shame and set you in a high place, secure and empowered to live and move, and have your being in My Spirit, far above all evil. So when the enemy accuses you or you feel inadequate after listening to his lies, speak My Word and say, "I am an overcomer, a child of the king, a member of the royal priesthood, covered by the blood of Jesus, so I render your words void, in the name of Jesus. You have to flee in terror, right now! So go!"

He Leads Me Beside Still Waters

Once you can believe what I have said about you, I will make you mighty and help you accomplish great feats by the power of My Holy Spirit—unshakable and fearless, as you stand in faith and trust Me for the days ahead. As you keep short accounts with Me and soak in My presence, letting Me change you day by day, we will become inseparable, and you will glorify Me as never before, by the power of My Spirit—sending up a sweet-smelling fragrance that even Heaven will stop to admire...

My Glorious Presence

"Cast me not away from thy presence; and take not thy holy spirit from me. Restore unto me the joy of thy salvation; and uphold me with thy free spirit." (Psalms 51:11-12)

My Precious Child,

In Psalms we see that my servant David asked me to search him and know his heart, to try him and know his thoughts to see if there was any wicked way in him. (Psalms 139: 23-24) He also cried out for Me to create in him a clean heart and restore to him the joy of his salvation. That's because he knew that the only place of rest for My children is when fellowship is sweet between us, and nothing hinders us from sharing our hearts. And because that's true, I desire to search your heart and allow my precious Holy Spirit to shine His gentle light on the dark places you have tried to hide out of shame. But don't let shame keep us apart. Refuse to let anything separate us.

David knew that his joy could only be restored through My glorious presence, (Ps. 51:12) so he cried out from deep within: **'Cast me not away from thy presence.'** He couldn't even imagine the emptiness of a life without my Holy Spirit. In the end, when David strayed he quickly ran back into My presence and repented, once again wrapping himself in the comfort of My waiting arms. And as his reward I wrapped him in My glory, and put a new song in his heart, restoring the joy of his salvation and giving him peace. After all, he was a man after my own heart!

I want you to know, my child, that My glorious presence is given to those who seek true restoration. I will cleanse you, purge your sins, and cast them as far as the east is from the west if you will only ask Me. However, I will not shine light upon the dark and hidden places unless you first give me permission, for I am a gentleman and I will never force myself on anyone. But if you will cry out to Me with all your heart, I will cleanse you and restore to you the joy found only in My glorious presence.

Understand what it means when I say that I made a way for you to enter the holy of holies. I am yours; you are Mine. And once you are restored to Me we will be in unity, moving as one. So come and abide in Me, and I in you, to do the will of the Father, and live out that glorious destiny you can only dream of . . .

Purity of Mind

"And now, dear brothers and sisters, one final thing. Fix your thoughts on what is true, and honorable, and right, and pure, and lovely, and admirable. Think about things that are excellent and worthy of praise." (Philippians 4:8)

My Precious Child,

Do you not know that replaying old, painful memories of your ruined past will only chain you to them? I never intended you to be a prisoner to yesterday. I see that you've collected old memories, storing them away in the far reaches of your mind only to play them again and again. Each replay drains your spirit of the joy and life I have given you. It literally squelches the anointing inside you.

So that Satan will not outsmart you, you must be familiar with his evil schemes! Do not allow him to beat you over the head with your past. Do not allow him to remind you of the painful hurts or failures of yesterday, for he is the accuser of the brethren! He attacks you with condemnation and guilt, dressing you in a garment of shame, and when he pronounces you incompetent, he steals the confidence you need to live for Me. He convinces you that you're too far gone—worthless. This, my child, is a lie!

I shed My blood for you so that every sin could be forgiven, so that all hurts and wounds could be healed by the stripes I took upon my back. I bled and died to set you free from every sin, wound and infirmity. My Word says to put the past behind you, and render it harmless in light of the cross, for I remember it not. As far as the East is from the West I have separated you from your sins, so why do you allow the enemy to pounce on you with his barrage of accusations? When he comes to accuse you, tell him he's got the wrong person, for that is not who you are anymore! I will have the last word! Take the authority I have already given you and live as if it is so. Choose to believe me, and not ugly lies of the enemy!

I have seen your tears and your shame, but I have forgiven you and now declare you righteous through My shed blood and your true repentance. You were as the prodigal wearing the robe of humiliation, smelling of filth, sin and regret, but My face was always turned toward you, waiting for you to repent and return to Me. When you took even a few steps toward Me, I had already started running to meet you—to embrace you as My precious child and dress you in a robe of righteousness, giving you a place of honor, and a brand new beginning.

So let go of the past! Let me destroy the chains that try to keep you captive to old, dead news that no longer applies to My beloved. Let Me pour My oil into your wounds and wash your mind, restoring purity of thought, a clean heart and renewed spirit. Fix your thoughts on Me and My Word. Let My fire consume you with divine love. For I am giving you a new mind that is focused on Me!

Throw away the old tapes of shame and humiliation that replay in your mind, and focus on a new set of truths—those that are true, and honorable, and right, and pure, and lovely, and admirable. When the enemy comes in to accuse you, refuse his lies, and rebut them with the truth, that you are a new creature in Me, and the old things have passed away. Tell him you will no longer listen to a single thing he says, because My opinion is the only one that matters, and I say you are a blood-washed saint, a powerhouse of faith whom God will use to change the world!

Never Give Up or Give in

"Do not throw away your confidence; it will be richly rewarded."
(Hebrews 10:13)

My Precious Child,

Did you know that when My Son, Jesus, left heaven to go to Earth in the form of a man, He gave up His deity, so that He was no more or less human than you are? In fact, He had left all His power in heaven, when an angel led Him out to the wilderness where He would stay for forty days and nights. It was an uncomfortable place, where He had no food, water or comfortable bed or place to rest. And yet Scripture says He didn›t complain. How did He accomplish that? He knew that, in order to fulfill His destiny, He had to develop patience in the face of things that most human beings would abhor or even refuse to endure.

This was true because He actually came to suffer, and who among you enjoys that? The truth is that no one does, but at times My plan will require things of you that aren›t comfortable or fun, yet they will serve My purpose and fulfill your destiny if you choose to bow to My will for you. And if it seems unloving for Me to do that, remember that I loved My Son, Jesus, more than life itself, yet I required Him to die a cruel death on a cross, taking your place, to buy you back from the hand of your enemy.

Those who truly belong to Me and love Me will want to be part of My strategic plan, whatever that involves. Are you in that place? How would you respond if I asked you to do something hard? Would you trust Me to make a way for you, providing for every need, and cheering you on every step of the way? Most people aren't willing, and if that's true, they aren't useful, and I must search for another to do My will. The choice is yours, but if you follow Me, you will receive great blessing and rich rewards. When you submit to My will, you release a sweet-smelling fragrance like none other, and I am pleased. How much do you want to please Me? I gently invite you to follow Me...

Getting to the Root

"He cuts off every branch in me that bears no fruit, while every branch that does bear fruit he prunes so that it will be even more fruitful." (John 15:2)

My Precious Child,

I see your heart is wounded and bruised, and you carry a burden too heavy to bear. The journey has been treacherous and long. You're stunned and angry, unable to believe it happened, and you wonder if your wounds will ever heal or if the pain will ever stop. I want you to know that it was I who molded your heart from clay, and it is I who hold the dirty, broken pieces and declare over you a new beginning. Place your fragmented heart in the palm of my hands, and trust Me to heal you and make you whole.

Your pain is clearly evident in your reactions, attitudes and the way you talk. The wounds are so deep that it colors everything else in your life and affects every response. In fact, it's become your identity, one you wear like a banner, to announce your right to be bitter. But that's not the way

I want you to live.

I want to get to the root cause of those traumatic wounds. I want to go to the source and heal and restore. I won't just cosmetically cover the scars... I am going to the root! I am going deeper than ever before. Why? Because I want my bride to be healthy, well-balanced and mature, without spot or wrinkle. In fact, I will heal **every wound** if you'll allow it, even the ones caused by others. The remarkable truth is that you no longer have to be a victim, scarred and incapacitated, stuck in the ravages of your past.

I want to heal those old, negative mindsets and reactions. I don't want you to walk through life with a broken spirit . . . trying to protect yourself and becoming increasingly more rigid, negative, and judgmental. Instead, I want you to have My mind and heart, quickly discarding the negative. In order to reflect God's love, we must not be on the defensive, always on guard, because that is not who I am. Rather be healed, and set free from negativity and judgment, so you can love freely. Allow Me to heal you and remove the walls of negativity that have been hallmarks in your life in the past, and replace them with love and compassion for those around you. Then, if problems arise you can simply cast those feelings upon Me and deal with the issues in mature, healthy ways.

As you let go of the things that hinder you, the chains of the past will fall away. Fear, anger, resentment and bitterness toward others will disappear as you are restored. I will redeem all of that if you let Me. Please, my child, don't start your day gazing in the rear view mirror with blame on your mind. Instead, give Me permission to address the root cause, so you can start afresh. Let me heal your mind, soul, and emotions so you can worship Me in spirit and in truth, withholding nothing. Trust again. Try Again. Take a hold of My hand. I love you and will never leave you the way you are if you let Me transform you.

In fact, let Me go a step further. If you think you can hold on to those old wounds and the bitterness that accompanies them, think again, because I will not support those who refuse the grace I freely offer. And to look at it another way, realize that wounds are open doors the devil walks through, to hinder and manipulate when you fail to forgive, refusing My healing touch.

Consider this: I want to pour out my spirit on all mankind, but until you let go of bitterness, I can do absolutely nothing. Did you hear that? Let me say it again—it's that important! **You actually prevent Me from going to work on your behalf when you fail to allow me into the dark, infected places of your heart.** Only as you repent of the need to hold on to them, and turn away from those old, sick ways of reacting, can I change your heart, heal your wounds, and make you new. The truth is that **you get to choose** whether or not to let go of the garbage that drags you down and keeps you in bondage.

This is a season of Great Preparation for the coming visitation of My presence to this lost, dark earth. I am preparing a bride who will be **humble, holy and intimate** with Me, her Groom. I will prune: that is expose, uproot, and cut off the dead branches in your life to make you that beautiful, mature bride. I will deal with the hidden things in your heart—not as a mean stepfather, but rather a loving Daddy who only desires to bring His prized child closer to himself. I am a holy God, so let go, and bury your past in the sea of forgetfulness. It's time to move on and live out your destiny. The choice is yours. What will you do?

He Leads Me Beside Still Waters

Freedom

"Around midnight Paul and Silas were praying and singing hymns to God, and the other prisoners were listening. 26Suddenly, there was a massive earthquake, and the prison was shaken to its foundations. All the doors immediately flew open, and the chains of every prisoner fell off!"
(Acts 16:25-26)

My Precious Child,

I am a God of freedom! My greatest desire is to set people free through My shed blood. However, Satan hates freedom and comes to bind and enslave those I love, in prisons of oppression, worry, fear, hate and lust, to name only a few. Many are in chains pleading for deliverance from that dark and lonely place, with no one to turn to for comfort or a way of escape. But I am here, and I am their way out.

Did you hear that? I am your way of escape! Even as I sent the earthquake to open the prison for Paul and Silas, I also desire to shake the ground and open your prison door by the power of My might.

Even as Peter saw his chains fall off and the metal gate that led into the city suddenly open, (Acts 12:7, 10) I want to open the gate of freedom in your life and shatter the chains that have kept you bound for years.

I came that you might have deliverance: I've given you authority over the enemy, so take hold of the vision and declare and decree your freedom, walking away from hopelessness and every sin that besets you. Stand in confidence and claim your freedom, asking Me for help, choosing to hate those evil habits and fight them off as enemies of your soul.

Stop speaking defeat over your life. When you say, "I'm impossible, I have this bondage or that bondage," you open the door for the enemy to make the situation worse. So stop believing what you see with your eyes, and believe what I say. Believe Me when I say you have power over turmoil, sickness, darkness, and every evil thing that oppresses you, because My death on the cross restored all that was lost in Eden. As you trust Me and begin to live as if it's so, believing I will make a way for everything you need, you'll be set free from even the most hopeless of prisons, and you will strip the enemy of his power.

Behold, "you're a new creature" in Me; through your union with Me, **'Old things are passed away and all things have become new.'** (2 Cor. 5:17) Paul said, **"I was crucified with Christ, nevertheless I live, yet not I, but Christ lives in me."** (Gal. 2:20) Let Me say it again—I live in you!

When you accepted My gift of salvation and were baptized, your old man was nailed to the cross and buried with Me to be raised up in newness of life, empowering you to live in a new way that brings honor to My name.

Just as death had no power over Me the enemy no longer has power over you because of My work on the cross. So consider yourself dead to sin and alive to Me, and see your shackles fall off so that you can exit your prison and once again walk on holy ground.

Right now I want you to say with all your heart:

Father God, I thank You that You've delivered me from the power of sin and the devil, so that my citizenship is now in the kingdom of light. I have been raised together with You, far above all principalities, powers, rulers of darkness of this world, and wicked spirits in high places. Sin no longer has power over me; rather I have dominion over sin. I am dead to sin and every evil thing, which is now under my feet, in Jesus' name!

The Ointment that Soothes all Pain

"If you forgive those who sinned against you, your heavenly Father will forgive you. But if you refuse to forgive others, your Father will not forgive your sins."
(Matthew 6:14-15)

My Precious Child,

Forgiveness releases My healing ointment that soothes every pain. I know you carry old wounds that haunt you to this day. Even the thought of them brings heartache and weeping. You've shared with me your bitter ordeal and I have lovingly listened to every detail, but now it's time for you to release to it to Me, so I can apply My soothing ointment and render powerless that pain.

But that can only happen if you choose to forgive those who hurt you. Perhaps that seems like too much to ask. If that's true, answer this question: How much do you want all I have to give? If you're ready to end your own desperate struggle, the process is simple; open your heart and let me take the bitterness and unforgiveness and touch you with My healing unction.

Let Me tell you a little secret: Holding on to your right to bitterness is like being attached to a stinking dead body that is in the process of decay. That attachment will eventually poison and steal the life from you. Is that a good trade-off? Of course not—it will eventually kill you. And if you want Me to bless and use you, you must let go of bitterness, let go of those desires for revenge, and let My love transform you from the inside out.

As you open your heart and release those hurts to me, I will touch them one by one and make the scars like baby-fresh skin, with no ugly flaw. I will anoint you with the oil of joy and put a new song in your heart, so that the pain is just a memory, and becomes a mighty testimony of My ability to free those who are bound. Once you're free, you become a thing of beauty and great joy to Me, a living example of My glory.

When your heart is broken and you feel like lashing out in your pain, run into My arms and dump it in My lap, for I alone have the words of healing that will set you free to once again soar in your spirit, untouched and unfettered by the cares of the world. Let Me give you the oil of joy to replace your grief, and a brand new song of victory—it's waiting for you to reach out and take it!

Be Careful What Grabs Your Heart

"And when the woman saw that the tree was good for food, and that it was pleasant to the eyes, and a tree to be desired to make one wise, she took of the tree, and did eat, and gave also unto her husband with her, and he did eat."
(Genesis 3:6)

My Precious Child,

I am your Creator, the one who loves you more than life itself. I am the only one worthy of your worship. So be on guard, because the enemy would love to seduce and beguile you, stealing your destiny just as he did with Adam and Eve.

It all began in the Garden where Adam and Eve had perfect communion with Me, We walked and talked in the cool of the day, and were the best of friends. I had only one stipulation: they were not to eat of the Tree of the Knowledge of Good and Evil, lest they die and be separated from Me forever.

Then, one day, Eve noticed how delicious the fruit looked on that tree, the only one forbidden. And the serpent appeared to her and coaxed her into tasting it, saying it would make her wise. At his invitation she allowed her heart to lust after what ultimately led to certain death. She took it in her hands and couldn›t resist the lies of the enemy.

The curse then was the result of focusing on and craving the wrong thing, believing it would make her complete. Now, as then, when people do their own thing they cut off my endless supply of life, once again making the sin of consequence a certainty.

So guard your heart, and focus on Me, allowing Me to lead and protect you from deception and sin. Be careful what you focus on, what you allow to grab your heart. Don›t hold close to you or dare to go near the unclean, forbidden thing, for over and over in My Word are sad tales of mighty warriors gone wrong, because they couldn›t stand firm and be strong.

Let Me grab your heart. Stop staring temptation in the face. Look away and make a covenant with your eyes, to focus on and worship only Me, and you will be favored beyond your wildest dreams!

Controlling Your Thought Life

"But clothe yourself with the Lord Jesus Christ (the Messiah), and make no provision for [indulging] the flesh [put a stop to thinking about the evil cravings of your physical nature] to [gratify its] desires (lusts)."
(Romans 13:14, AMP)

My Precious Child,

I see a war raging *for* your mind, *in* your mind. Until he's defeated, the enemy will fight until he controls your thoughts and thereby impacts your actions. He thinks he's crafty as he comes to plant ideas in your mind, seducing you to dwell on his plans for evil instead of My plans for good. Remember, My Word says to guard your hearts and minds from the enemy's tactics.

If you desire to live at your full potential you must control your thoughts, or they will control you. I want you to know that not every thought that comes your way is worthy of your attention; you have free will to accept or reject thoughts, so learn to discern the source. Evil thoughts do not originate in the regenerated mind of a believer whose mind remains on Me. They come from an outside source, so do not beat yourself up for having them, simply reject them and the one who sends them.

Thoughts are like seeds, and you water them by giving them room to grow in the garden of your mind. What seeds are you planting there—seeds of faith, hope, victory and strength, or those of doubt, unbelief, disappointment and failure?

Many of My children are being robbed of their future because their thinking is out of harmony with My plans for them. They meditate on thoughts of lust and greed, idolizing the things of the world, and thereby walk away from their destiny.

I'm calling My children to saturate themselves in the Word, so that they have My mind rather than being double minded, straddling the fence, with carnal living. Seek to be holy as I am holy; refuse to dwell on the past or on negative possibilities, speaking only life words and Scripture over your lives, because you get what you say. Start declaring My promises, claiming what I've said, so fear and dread will flee, and you will begin to reckon yourselves dead to sin, which will no longer hold any appeal.

I am calling you to victory over your thought life. I don't want you to remain a prisoner to negative thinking and hopelessness! I have come to set you free, and the battle will be won. Do not be afraid to ask Me for help, do not be ashamed to bring to Me every thought. I am always here when you need Me. You will keep in perfect peace him whose mind is steadfast, because he trusts in you. (See Isaiah 26:3)

You cannot fight this battle alone, so humble yourself before Me. Walk away from evil things; submit to My will for you. Ask for help from trustworthy, godly people, and I will purify your mind so you can live in victory. Renew your mind with My Word and saturate yourself in My presence, for in the process, all evil and negative thinking will fall away. Let Me purify your mind and make you holy as I am holy.

Pray as King David did long ago:

"Search me, O God, and know my heart;

test me and know my thoughts.

Point out anything in me that offends you,

and lead me along the path of everlasting life."

(Psalm 139:23-24, NLT)

You are no longer a victim of your past; you are a brand new creation in Me (see 2 Corinthians 5:17), because of My miraculous work on the cross.

Old strongholds can be shattered. Patterns of negative thinking and behavior are learned, and they can be unlearned in My presence and by meditating on My Word.

How badly do you want to win? Victory is truly yours if you're ready to let go of everything that is not of Me. Your victory awaits—will you come to Me, run to Me, and refuse to accept less than My best for you? Don't wait another minute!

Contending

"Hear ye now what the Lord saith; Arise, contend thou before the mountains and let the hills hear thy voice."
(Micah 6:1)

My Precious Child,

You're in a spiritual battle, and the kingdom of darkness wants you to let go of the dreams and purposes that I've called you to. He wants to prevent you from reaching new levels in the spirit, to hinder your advancement and stop the flow of the anointing in your life. You have become weary in the fight, and sometimes it appears that the enemy has won. But that is a lie; right now I declare over you that he will not succeed!

It is I who called you and placed those dreams in your heart, and it is I who will bring about your kingdom purposes. Allow Me to fight your battles for you as you come into agreement with My will for your life. (Exodus 14:14)

At the same time, I want you to know that dreams don't always fall in your lap ... you must contend for your breakthrough. I have called you to 'contend'! Let this word resound so loudly within you that you can't ignore it. To **contend** means to defend, assert, claim, insist, declare, profess, and affirm. The battle is mine, but you must come into agreement with it and decree it on Earth as it is in heaven in order to make it reality.

Yes, I could easily hand those things to you ... but I strengthen you in the process of contending, giving you the authority to take back that which was stolen. I want you to rise up and take the ground I've given you.

Stand up and declare to the mountains that I am your God! Don't let their size intimidate you; say to that mountain of lack, that mountain of failure, that mountain of insecurity, "Be removed by the power of His might!" Affirm your reliance on Me, and watch the mountains shrink into molehills before you.

The battle is raging around you, so I need you to **rise up, and stand against the enemy, decreeing and confirming in the Spirit what rightfully belongs to you.** In order for you to overcome the enemy you must wage war in the heavens by verbally proclaiming your right to live out the destiny to which I've called you.

I know you sense my Spirit all around you, declaring over you new beginnings, new dimensions, new associations, and new spheres of influence, amid resistance and oppression. But you must wage war

for your future, because your next level hangs in the balance. This is the way Timothy felt when Paul told him to fight the good fight of faith (See 1 Tim. 6:12).

Exercise your spiritual authority in My name whenever the **enemy tries to defraud you of My promises. He has come to discourage and frustrate you—to trample you underfoot, and make you miscarry what I am birthing in your life—to make you miss your appointment with destiny by dis-appointing you.**

In essence, the enemy works to get you ousted from your new position and future promotion. That's why you need to contend! I want to encourage you to keep declaring My Word over your life, and refuse to be defrauded.

The truth is that your battle is not in the natural, so refuse to contend with your boss, spouse, children, sister, brother, church members or friends. In fact, Ephesians 6:12 puts it this way:

"For we are not wrestling with flesh and blood [contending only with physical opponents], but against the despotisms, against the powers, against [the master spirits who are] the world rulers of this present darkness, against the spirit forces of wickedness in the heavenly (supernatural) sphere." (AMP)

Now that doesn't mean we're to be obsessed with the devil, searching for him around every corner, but it does mean that we are not to be deceived, because he is like a roaring lion, pacing back and forth looking to devour the weak and vulnerable. Rather we are to draw near to God in worship and obedience, getting in unity with His purpose, and then using our authority to speak into being the will of God for our lives.

Our battles are won in the spirit, but you must learn to discern the tactics of the enemy to know what you're up against. Remain vigilant and alert and use wise battle strategies against him (1 Tim. 1:18). Ask me to teach you to war (Ps. 144:1), for in the process you will experience promotion and kingdom advancement. The strategy for today is: "Contend!"

Protect your calling and reach for new heights, Don't fall for the snares of the enemy, Stand strong, Mighty Warrior!

Steve Porter

Little Foxes that Spoil the Vine

"Catch all the foxes. Those little foxes before they ruin the vineyard of love for the grapevines are blossoming."
(Song of Solomon 2:15, NLT)

My Precious Child,

There is profound truth in this statement: the life is found in the vine. Just as nourishment goes out to all the branches, so that beautiful fruit will mature, so **'I am the Vine and you are the branches.'** (John 15:5) The best nourishment comes from abiding as close as possible in Me, so that My life can fill you to overflowing with the abundant life and beautiful fruit.

The flow of that life occurs when you saturate yourself in My presence, through prayer, studying My Word, and fasting. When you live out of that abundant flow it makes the enemy very nervous, and he will stop at nothing to hinder the flow of the Spirit in your life. He knows that most will not fall for larger, more obvious distractions so he uses 'little things' that might go unnoticed, hoping you'll take his bait.

You know well how little things can come up that steal your time with Me. They are the little foxes that the Bible talks about. The point is that little, seemingly insignificant things can ultimately cause huge damage. So be on guard against little foxes that wreak havoc in the life of a believer.

Notice I said 'little foxes' and not big foxes, as the little ones are able to sneak in and out of the vines and nip at them secretly, to damage or steal the fruit. My children, I have called you to a deeper, more meaningful relationship with Me. The truth is that, every day, things happen to prevent you from going deeper with Me. I want you to be able to stand up to the distractions and say, "I will pay no attention to that. I refuse to even consider that. I will let nothing steal My time with God. Leave now, every distraction, in Jesus' name!"Little foxes matter to Me. They sneak in almost unnoticed to short-circuit our fellowship. They are mundane distractions that come before Me, consuming your time and attention. Do not forget, as well, that little foxes grow into big foxes.

'Little foxes' can also be seen as 'little sins' or 'little habits' that slowly suck the life found in Me from you.

Such tiny cracks always grow bigger: the fine line in the instrument grows wider, so the music is off key. When a dike springs even the smallest leak, it grows under the pressure behind it, until it becomes a flood that destroys everything in its wake. My point is that you must never allow yourself to excuse even the briefest sinful behavior or habit, but see each one as a thief. With that in mind, always choose to bow your mind and heart in obedience to Me, and seek My face exclusively, setting everything else aside. In so doing, you will walk in the fullness of My presence.

Sin is sin, so don't be fooled. In the end, sin cripples you, preventing you from running the race I've set before you. **Those little foxes love to spoil tender young grapes; those new beginnings in your life, those anointed births or starts.** And if you grow cold, you won't even care.

So what are the first signs of little foxes taking ground in My vineyard? When your heart drifts from me and even the Living Word can't break through. When that to-do list consumes all your attention, squeezing out every thought of Me. When you go through the motions, without ever touching My heart. When it becomes little more than a habit and loses its appeal, so that you no longer miss Me at all. When you excuse sin as 'not that bad'.

When you see those things happening, be grief-stricken and weep, for you've grown cold, and the enemy has stolen My most precious gifts, which means you must run, run, run to my cross to repent, and return to your first love.

Don't let the devil win by diverting your attention from Me. He wants to abort your precious calling and destroy your destiny, so be on guard and let nothing distract you from My secret place.

Check your heart: is the flame of passion hotter than ever?

Or is it dying out? If it's burning lower, fuel the flame by throwing yourself at My feet and holding on for dear life, for your destiny is at stake. Let nothing, nothing, nothing deter you from the secret place. Use the authority I've given you to expel every little fox, and guard your heart, knowing the devil can never win when you love Me best.

Oaks of Righteousness

"They may be called oaks of righteousness, the planting of the Lord, that he may be glorified. They shall build up the ancient ruins; they shall raise up the former devastations; they shall repair the ruined cities, the devastations of many generations."
(Isaiah 61: 3-4)

My Precious Child,

I see the long wait through which you›ve been struggling and I am touched by your infirmities, You›ve stood firm and held on to My promises through many heartaches, believing for a breakthrough, yet at times you›ve been tempted to give up. I›ve heard you ask, «Lord, how long?» but I want to encourage you to look at them through the eyes of heaven. I see the bigger picture; those challenges are making you strong. I know the outcome—I see you as an overcomer, faithful and victorious to the end. I understand that you›re ready for the pressure to stop, but refuse to short-circuit the process until I am ready, and trust Me until then.

Consider the oak. A tiny acorn falls to the ground and breaks open to take root. Notice that it grows quite slowly. At first its roots are shallow and its trunk is narrow, but then come the storms and winds and heat that make it stronger over time, and its roots grow deeper until, one day, that oak is a beautiful and mighty tree, that stands strong in the face of the most devastating stormy winds. It spreads protective leafy arms over the earth, providing shade and shelter from the relentless heat. Its roots hold water and prevent soil erosion. It›s a thing of beauty to behold.

In the same way, you are a thing of beauty to behold, growing strong, standing firm in the face of trouble. You can be confident that I love you and will never leave, for I abide in you, closer than a brother. Call upon Me and I will answer and strengthen you, encouraging you and cheering you on, until the process is complete. And one day soon you will look back and be glad, and your reward will be great, for I Am is proud of you, like a father who can boast about his precious, amazing child. You are Mine, so never, never give up. Just trust that I know best, and will provide all you need to make it through to victory.

Steve Porter

He Leads Me Beside the Still Waters

He makes me to lie down in green pastures; He leads me beside the still waters. He restores my soul;
Psalms 23:2-3a

My Precious Child,

Do not fight it when I call you away from the draw of earthly distractions. Do not resist My wooing to come away, because busyness can lead to a dry place, where your spirit is no longer sensitive to My voice. Can you hear Me calling--inviting you to an oasis where My living water always flows and My face shines upon your weary soul? It's there that I renew you and cause you to grow--where I reveal My presence to you in a fresh new way.

I'm calling you away, to hide you in My secret place--to give you a time of rest so that you can recharge. And though it goes against the grain to rest, that's exactly what I designed you to do. Resist the temptation to exit My presence prematurely lest you leave without everything I want to give you--wisdom and direction that will fill you up and bless everything you do. Don't give into anxiety or fear or allow yourself to be uncomfortable or awkward, for there you're in My perfect will, and I am jealous over you. Let Me take you away to that gentle stream of refreshment.

I have many things to share to you from deep within My heart, but you will only hear them as you quiet your heart, and listen for My still, small voice. Today I'm calling you to a higher place in Me, and making you desperate for Me. In that secret place I will share My heart with you, and reveal Myself in ways you won't discover any other way.

In this place even the wounds of your past will heal and I will reveal My will. I'll show you how these things work together to mature you. In this place you will be empowered by My anointing. Only commune with Me; share your heart with Me, and let Me fill you with the living water that never runs dry. There I will refresh you so you no longer thirst again for anything but Me.

Seek solitude and listen in the silence, for only there will you sense My nearness. Only there will I reveal Myself, in order to teach you and strengthen you with priceless treasures of wisdom and understanding that can't be found anywhere else. It is there that I will restore your soul.

If you don't sense My nearness when you sit in silence, do not budge, for I often veil My face and hide My presence so you will seek Me by faith and not by feelings. And though you do not see Me, understand that My abiding presence is always there, and that I will calm your spirit, giving you rest as you lay your head upon My lap and let Me touch your very heart.

My Brooding Presence

«O Jerusalem, Jerusalem, who kills the prophets, and stones those who are sent to you; how often would I have gathered your children together, as a hen does gather her brood under her wings, and you would not.» (Luke 13:34)

My Precious Child,

My heart is so tender toward you. I delight in making you strong and successful in the Spirit. Just as a mother hen instinctively sits upon her eggs in order to bring forth a new generation, I hover over you with My wings, protectively covering you. In the same way, the Holy Spirit broods over those who need His comfort and protection.

I promised Israel: **'My presence shall go with thee, and I will give thee rest.'** (Exodus 33:14) And the same is true for you.

Such a promise is designed to send a yearning deep into your being, knowing there is a brooding presence hovering over you that defies human word and thought.

The manifestation of My presence was wondrous as I hovered over the children of Israel in the wilderness, in a pillar of fire or a pillar of cloud. In fact, Psalm 121:5-6 says this: **'The Lord is thy Keeper; the Lord is thy shade upon thy right hand. The sun shall not smite thee by day, nor the moon by night. The Lord shall preserve thee from all evil.'**

Psalm 16:1 goes on to say: **'Thou wilt shew me the path of life; in Thy presence is fullness of joy; at Thy right hand there are pleasures for evermore.'**

And while you may not see a visible "cloud" of My presence, My Word gives you confidence that I will never leave you or forsake you. (Hebrews 13:5)

Wherever you go, I am there, anticipating your arrival. I have already made the way straight, before you even ask. So comfort yourselves, no matter what you see with your natural eyes—I am always with you and in you, to keep, cover, nourish, protect and lead you from victory to victory. Grab hold of the truth, and wrap it around you, as your shield and buckler, for **I Am** has already made it happen...

Eye of the Dove

"Behold, you are fair, My love! behold, you are fair! You have dove's eyes."
(Song of Solomon 1:15)

My Precious Child,

Beloved, I am calling you to a far deeper relationship with Me, to focus your gaze on Me alone. Even as a dove fixes its gaze upon its mate, unmoved by distractions, even so, I want you to fix your gaze on Me alone, My 'love bird'.

Do not be like a horse or a mule easily distracted by side-vision. It can only be kept on track by placing 'blinders' beside each eye, and a bit in its teeth.

Unlike the horse or mule, stubborn and easily distracted, I want you to be like that 'love bird' with singular purpose, focusing dove eyes on Me so I can lead you according to My will.

Love me enough to be obedient, allowing your spirit to become ever more sensitive to My still, small voice. I will lead you to safety, shelter, and protection—only trust Me and allow Me to guide your steps. Stay close enough to Me to sense My will for you. With one tender glance I will send you in the right direction, where you will find favor and spiritual substance.

'I will instruct you and teach you in the way you should go; I will guide you with My eye.' (Psalm 32:8)

As your *'dove's eyes'* focus on Me I will bring a greater awareness of My presence. I will begin to minister to you in a very personal way and lift you far above the pull of this evil world, giving you a new sensitivity to My Spirit.

How much do you love Me? Can I trust you to develop a singular focus on Me alone so that you do not miss My best? Will you gaze upon Me only, leaving behind all others and the things that so tantalize you now? Once you fall in love with My face, you'll no longer be satisfied to merely hear *about* Me; rather you'll yearn for My presence, eager to be in My company, where I will satisfy the deep longings inside you.

With that 'singular gaze' will also come a change in your desires. I will quench your cravings for the things of this world and inspire you to come away with Me.

'Rise up, My love, My fair one, and come away.' (Song of Solomon 2:10)

I yearn for you to have only one desire—to abide in My holy presence. I long for you to stay in My presence and never leave, no matter what else occupies your time.

Cry out even as David:

'The Lord is my light and my salvation; whom shall I fear? ... <u>one thing have I desired of the Lord,</u> **that will I seek after; that I may dwell in the house of the Lord all the days of my life, to behold the beauty of the Lord, and to inquire in His temple.'** (Psalm 27:1-4)

As you let Me stir your passion for Me, getting back to your first love, I will supply every need, filling you to overflowing, and far surpassing your expectations—finally giving you that elusive abundant life.

'But seek ye first the Kingdom of God and His righteousness; and all these things shall be added unto you.' (Matthew 6:33)

Today, I search earnestly for those who are willing to be doves with that kind of singleness of vision. When I find them it brings Me incredible joy, so that I can't help but declare:

'Behold, you are fair, you have dove's eyes.' (Song of Solomon 1:15)

Once I know you love Me most, more than great wealth, more than any other—once I have become to you a sought-after pearl of great price, I will be your fairest of ten thousand. I am altogether lovely, for I am your King of Kings and Lord of Lords, your All in All. Let me bring you to the banqueting house, where my banner over you is love!

Ask. Seek. Knock

"And so I tell you, keep on asking, and you will receive what you ask for. Keep on seeking, and you will find. Keep on knocking, and the door will be opened to you."
(Luke 11:9)

My Precious Child,

Did you know there is power in persistence when you knock, keep on knocking, and don't give up? Don't grow tired… Keep going strong, believing I will move on your behalf. When you ask, keep on asking. Don't waver or doubt, and when you seek, continue on in relentless pursuit believing Me for My promises. Refuse to grow weary in well doing, for I am with you. And remember that anything worth having is worth pursuing with all your heart.

Why would I ask you to be persistent? Because I want to know whether you really want Me or merely the things I provide. Are your priorities right? Are your motives pure? 'Seeking' often reveals the intentions of the heart. Is it just something you ask for occasionally? Are you halfhearted or apathetic in your quest?

I want you to be passionate and persistent in seeking Me. Come to Me for what you need and be persistent, refusing to take no for an answer, because you know the love of the Father. And if I don't answer right away, I will in due time if you continue to ask, seek, and knock.

If you desire to give good gifts to your children, how much more I, as your Heavenly Father, desire to give good gifts to you. I never let My children go hungry. I'm not a father who pushes them away or enjoys watching them beg and plead. As you quiet your soul and establish your heart, persistently standing in faith, the answer will come.

I'm not a loveless spectator who sits there and simply watches you perform. You are My sheep, and I am your Shepherd. I will not be deaf to your cry for help. I will deepen your faith and instruct you as you listen to Me and patiently wait. In the waiting you will find that you're being changed into My likeness, and becoming more sensitive to Me.

Persistent faith means asking, seeking, and knocking. That's what it's all about—a godly determination not to quit and throw in the towel. As long as what you ask for is within My perfect will, you can be assured that, if you keep on asking, keep on seeking, and keep on knocking— you will eventually receive the promise.

I already know what you need. Most of the time I don't instantly provide your needs, because My goal is to build a closer relationship with you. As you come to Me in sweet communion and ask and share your heart with Me it builds intimacy. Be relentless and persistent, until you feel a release in your spirit. And don't forget to thank Me for the answer even before you see the answer, because that is expectant faith in action. Be just as relentless in pursuing Me as I am relentless in loving you. And in the process you'll find everything you could ever imagine, because the deeper abundant life is found only as you seek Me.

Holy Desperation

"Who touched me?" Jesus asked.
When they all denied it, Peter said, "Master, the people
are crowding and pressing against you."
But Jesus said, "Someone touched me; I know that
power has gone out from me."
Luke 8:45-46

My Precious Child,

Consider this question: Have you been feeding on the garbage of the world for so long that you've lost your desperation for Me? Many who are supposed to belong to Me live day to day without an ounce of passion for Me, with little more than an empty, intellectual grasp, and no connection to My heart. But it's time for that to change. I'm calling you to a place of holy desperation before Me, for I long to hear you cry out to Me with all your heart. I long to see you lay prostrate before Me with your arms open wide, asking Me to touch you once more.

It has always been Satan's ploy to keep you so full of the junk of this world that you're no longer desperate for Me and My presence. Don't give into his distractions; don't let him pull you into apathy, but let Me woo you back to your first love, and stir up the dying embers inside you that long for more of Me.

Many of My children only go through the motions, praying halfhearted prayers, which is why they see no answers. I want you to fall in love with Me again, to cry out with a fresh desperation for Me. I will not turn away a heart that's on fire with love for Me.

Consider the woman with the issue of blood. Her desperation tapped into My power with a breakthrough faith that compelled her to elbow her way through the crowd to get to Me. She was pale and weak, having suffered twelve years with uterine bleeding. Doctors could not help her; instead of getting better she grew worse.

She knew I was her only hope. Even in her weakened state she refused to give up hope that I could heal her. So desperate was her need that she continued to pursue Me until she finally reached the place where I stood.

She had decided in her heart, "If I can just touch His clothes, I'll be healed" (Mark 5:28). Until that moment she'd been hopeless, but a tiny seed of hope had begun to bloom inside her. **Her illness had made her an outcast, unclean and untouchable, yet in the end, her faith made her whole. And I am still a God of restoration today.**

Even as she touched the edge of my cloak and I instantly felt the tug of her faith, I will take notice when you reach out and touch My heart. She was instantly healed by the virtue that flowed from within Me, and you too will be healed as you dare to reach out and touch Me with desperate faith.

Would your faith be enough to **constrain** Me? By that I mean would your case "compel, urge, or press with urgency"? Do you consider Me so precious and rare that you refuse to leave My side, no longer satisfied with a casual encounter or an intellectual grasp of who I am? Your desperate faith is what draws Me close in a way nothing else can. So will you reach out to Me and refuse to take no for an answer?

I will not walk past a heart that desperately constrains Me to come. I will make My habitation with you when you truly pursue Me with all your heart in faith. Cry out with all your heart, mind and strength; call out My name and I will come and minister to the needs of your heart.

Even as I said in Jeremiah 29:12-13 "In those days when you pray, I will listen. If you look for me wholeheartedly, you will find me."

I sometimes allow circumstances to stir up a desperate search for Me, so that I can display My power to fulfill your greatest need—for Me.

The truth is that none of these things will make sense to you until you search for Me as you would search for silver, until you seek Me as you would hidden treasure. Only then will you find everything you need in Me. For I am the true riches, and in Me, you will find hope, healing, restoration, revelation and ultimately—peace.

Beholding and Becoming

"We all, with unveiled face, beholding as in a mirror the glory of the Lord, are being transformed into the same image..."
(2 Corinthians 3:18)

My Precious Child,

My greatest desire is for you to be completely open and honest before Me so I can purify you, so that your life will become a mirror in which others can see Me. When the Spirit fills you, you are transformed, reflecting My glory—My character. Can't you tell when others have been in My presence, beholding the very glory of God, as your spirit senses My nature in them?

Keep your life open to me. Take a break from everything else. The busyness of things delays and hinders our time together. In order to live this way, you must keep your focus on Me, staying in unity with Me. Let other things come and go; let other people criticize you as they will; but never allow anything to detract from the life that "is hidden with me in God." Never stop abiding in Me, for this is the source of your power. It's not easy to focus on Me that closely, but it's possible and I will make it so as you stir up the passion within you for the things of God. Learn how to continue "beholding as in a mirror the glory of the Lord..." and put Me first, so that everything else fades in comparison.

To behold Me is to become like Me. As you sit in My presence and take in my beauty and splendor, I shine My face upon you. My reflection is then imprinted upon you. My face becomes your face! You are continually being conformed to My image.

To put it another way, as an elderly man sat in front of a primitive camera on a wooden tripod, the image of his weathered face imprinted itself on the glass inside the lightless chamber. The very same thing happens continually in the soul of every human being. This man's heart is much like the camera, and everything that passes before his eyes makes an imprint on his soul. I want to imprint My image upon your soul so that your very countenance reflects My beauty.

As this occurs you will become radiant with humble gentleness, glowing purity, and kindhearted compassion, offering patience and love for injustice, forgiving even your worst enemies. And just as I gave you an example of tender love and compassion when I went to the cross, you will follow My example as you behold Me.

Meditate on my love for you, as you gaze lovingly upon Me, and let Me quiet your fearful soul. And in the process you will be transformed to closely resemble Me. The glory of My face changes even the countenance of those who allow Me to move and shine through them. Others will recognize that, because of My presence, you've become clean and holy—you've been changed, reflecting My beauty.

Don't just glance upon me now and then, and don't be in a hurry just to catch a brief glimpse of Me, but fix your eyes on upon Me continuously. Bask in My presence and let me change and fill you. As you discipline yourself to behold me daily, My image will burn itself into your soul, so hold steady and train your spiritual eyes to focus on Me. Start today!

Get into your secret place that is set apart for Me alone. Close your eyes and quiet your mind and just love on Me. Allow your love for Me to well up within you and hold that love and affection out as a gift to Me. You will then begin to sense My presence stirring deep inside you, drawing you closer. Choose to rest and bask in that warm, loving place. It is there that I begin to make you look just like Me, reflecting My glory. Don't be in a hurry, for this love exchange can last for some time.

Like a sculptor who takes a rough piece of marble and begins to chisel away sections, he brings out the exquisite form in his mind's eye. The marble will not carve itself; the transformation happens over time through patience and hard work. In the same way you cannot change yourself—it's a work of the Holy Spirit that happens when you fix your eyes on upon Me while My glory streams down and brands its own dazzling imprint on your heart.

Consider the delicate flowers that turn toward the sun and focus on its warmth and light, slowly opening their buds to display their beauty; you must fix your gaze upon Me and allow the warmth of My love to saturate you. Such changes will not happen overnight. In fact, at first you may only notice the faintest of changes, the smallest glimpse of My beauty, but little by little you will become My masterpiece, displaying unspeakable joy, peace that flows like a river, a true humble spirit, and deep compassion for others. My divine attributes will shine through you.

Keep in mind that a mirror image is only an imperfect representation of the original, just as murky puddles only dimly reflect the glory of a landscape. More often than not, our lives resemble murky puddles the same way a cracked mirror inadequately reflects the face of the one holding it.

At times our lives are more like a cracked, distorted looking glass that reveals only tiny glimpses of the beauty it should reflect. In fact, the back of the mirror has no reflective qualities at all, even when turned toward the sun; the person holding it must gaze at the glass in order to see his reflection.

If you want to reflect My glory, you must keep your gaze continually on My face. Truly, the outcome is sure—as you spend time basking in My presence, you will begin to look like Me, and when others see you, they'll know you have been with Me, because My glory will shine through you, impacting the world for Me.

Praying and Singing the Scriptures

"This Book of the Law shall not depart from your mouth, but you shall meditate on it day and night, so that you may be careful to do according to all that is written in it. For then you will make your way prosperous, and then you will have good success."
(Joshua 1:8, ESV)

My Precious Child,

I'm calling you to take pleasure in receiving revelation from the Holy Scriptures. Chew on Scripture day and night and you will be as a tree replanted in Eden bearing fresh fruit every month—never dropping a single leaf, always in blossom. (See Psalms 1:2 MSG) There is such power in My Word—as you take time to carefully reflect and ponder the Holy Scriptures I have given you, I will heal you, restore you, and fill you to overflowing.

As I breathe on you My life-breath, My Word will open up to you as never before. You will feast and be satisfied by the marvelous spiritual banquet I prepared just for you. It's not about quantity or speed, but the attitude with which you read and pray the Scriptures. Little will be gained by rushing through it out of obligation.

So try this: When you turn to a passage I've led you to read, ask the Holy Spirit to reveal the deeper meaning behind the words on the page. Be careful to read it slowly, taking it all in, and contemplating its meaning. When you begin to sense My presence, linger in that moment and allow Me to reveal Myself to you from that verse.

Praying the Scripture is a spirit-led approach to reading the Word. But, as previously mentioned, it can't be done in a hurry. In fact, it's good to read it aloud, so that it goes through the ear-gate then through the mind and spirit. Refuse to speed through one passage to the next, until you sense the heart of what I mean. Then speak that passage back to Me in prayer, making it a petition, in worship. At that point, I will reveal to you things you've never known.

My Holy Spirit will be your teacher and will reveal hidden gems of truth, hidden manna, and nuggets of wisdom from the Word. You will extract new truths as I begin to reveal My heart to you, treasures not found anywhere else. Don't be like a bumble bee that simply flies by, scarcely touching the flower. Rather you must saturate yourself in My Word, so that it penetrates deep into your spirit, and its revelation begins to transform you.

As you wait before Me, resting in My presence, be aware of your spirit, and resist distractions that will try to come against you. If you wait on Me, I will break through for you and fill you with great joy and a sense of expectancy, believing Me for great things. Drink deeply of My Word in the secret place, and let Me satisfy the cravings within you.

Did you know that you can also sing the Scriptures to Me in worship? You open the Word and begin to sing the verses back to Me. Sing about who I am, what I've done, and don't forget to remind Me of My promises. Don't worry about how well you sing. I am listening for the cry of your heart rather than the quality of your voice, so don't try to impress Me—just show Me how much you love Me. Every song is a delight to My ears, a sacrifice of praise, a sweet fragrance that blesses My heart.

Praying and singing the Scriptures brings growth and healing into your life. My Word is alive and powerful. I desire to quicken it to you—to make it come alive within you and transform you and your circumstances—to see you grow into My likeness verse by verse. I will heal you as you pray and sing My Word. I will restore you with a personal word I quicken to your heart. I will rescue you from apathy and defeat and stir the embers of the fire that's died within you. I will visit you in ways you never imagined, as you drink deeply of the water of life found in My holy Word.

Eternal Weight of Glory

"For our light affliction, which is but for a moment, worketh for us a far more exceeding and eternal weight of glory"
(2 Corinthians 4:17, KJV)

My Precious Child,

When you think of a bride in the natural sense, you probably think of a mature woman who has reached a place, both emotionally and physically, where she's able and willing to marry. But how did she arrive at that place of maturity?

She arrived by persevering through various hardships. She stumbled and got back up again; she made mistakes and made them right, no matter what the cost.

In the same way, I'm looking for a fully mature bride who's been tested by fire and emerged as pure gold. Maturity comes through trials, which are a necessary part of growth. And growth means learning from mistakes—whether they're your own or someone else's. For instance, it usually doesn't take long for a young child to learn by experience that hot stoves burn little hands. But seldom do they take the advice of other, wiser people who try to protect them. Often, they choose to test the theory when no one is looking, by touching the hot stove and being burned. In the end, however, it is the pain, and not the protection of loving parents, that makes an unforgettable impact.

Consider the Apostle Paul, who wrote most of the New Testament. He's a great example of how the process of maturity comes through hardship. Paul describes some of his struggles in 2 Corinthians 11:23-28, and while he also suffered with an ongoing thorn in his side, My grace was always sufficient for him!

It's clear that, at the outset, Paul had a few issues remaining, yet he was clearly transformed by the challenges he endured. In spite of all the pain he suffered, he is single-handedly responsible for the ready availability of a large chunk of the Holy Book you hold in your hand today, almost 2,000 years later, through which I speak to you. I was always with him and My grace and anointing were available through it all.

And even though his struggles were ongoing, Paul chose not to become bitter. In fact, in Philippians 1:21 he said this: **"For to me to live *is* Christ, and to die *is* gain."**

The truth is that he increased in patience and maturity though all his many hardships. He was learning to die daily to himself and to allow Me to take first place on the throne of his life. And because he grew in grace, I could trust him to pick up his pen and write most of the New Testament, to speak only what I instructed, making clear My plans for the salvation of all mankind.

But Paul didn't just wake up one morning and say, "Hey, Jesus, how about giving me Your Word for all of mankind today?" He was tested and tried through the fire until he had learned to trust Me in everything. No matter what trials came his way, he realized there was a higher purpose for the suffering I allowed.

Philippians 3:14—**"I press toward the mark for the prize of the high calling of God in Christ Jesus. "**

Paul also made it a point to press forward toward this goal: (Philippians 3:10) **"That I may know him, and the power of his resurrection, and the fellowship of his sufferings, being made conformable unto his death."**

He realized that, in order to be like Me, he had to surrender all; to truly know Me, he had to face hardship. Paul embraced suffering in order to be transformed into My likeness. The truth is that Christ-likeness does not come easily or cheaply! He understood the higher purpose of hardship and welcomed it. In 2 Timothy 4:7-8 we see how Paul achieved this goal:

"<u>I have fought a good fight</u>, **I have finished *my* course, I have kept the faith: Henceforth there is laid up for me a crown of righteousness, which the Lord, the righteous judge, shall give me at that day: and not to me only, but unto all them also that love his appearing."**

At that point he was ready to be offered: In 2 Timothy 4:6 we read:

"For I am now ready to be offered, and the time of my departure is at hand."

He had gone through the maturing process, completed his work, and encouraged us as we endure our own afflictions:

2 Timothy 4:5— **"But watch thou in all things, endure afflictions, do the work of an evangelist, make full proof of thy ministry**. "

As a result of his trials, Paul realized that knowing and serving Me was worth more than life itself. In fact, he desired to be conformed into My image at any cost. He embraced the fire and let it do its work in him. The truth is that Paul's faithfulness earned him the crown of righteousness that I will give him; it will not just be handed to him on a silver platter. My salvation is a free gift, but your level of placement in My kingdom is up to you; your passionate faithfulness will be duly rewarded. And while your salvation is not won by good works, those who love Me little will never hear the wonderful phrase, "Well done, thou good and faithful servant." If you have loved and served Me well and give Me first place, I will smile on you and will bless you.

In the same way, a life of ease, although convenient, may not always be the best thing for you either. Please trust in My integrity, knowing that I know best, and your maturity is My goal. In the end I'm more interested in your character than your comfort—creating a masterpiece filled with fierce determination who will dare to do great things for Me. Don't settle for 'easy street', but work hard and embrace the struggle because without it you will never be strong enough to live out your destiny. Whether you realize it or not there is an eternal weight of glory in your struggles. As you endure the trials you face I'm working in you an inner wealth that exceeds the value of great riches. As you allow Me to prune you, willingly crucifying your flesh and surrendering your will to Mine, I will reveal Myself to you in ways you could never dream of. At that point I will be your everything, so that you wouldn't exchange My gift for anything.

2 Timothy 2:3— **'Thou therefore endure hardness, as a good soldier of Jesus Christ.'**

Mighty warrior, you mature not only by reading the Word and by prayer, but by the hardships you face every day. But no matter what struggles you face, call on Me, so I can make a way for you, for through Me you will be more than a conqueror. My grace will always be more than enough to take you through to victory.

The weight of temporary afflictions is feather light, while the glory before us is a thing of substance, something eternal that will never pass away. If Paul could describe his trials as light and momentary, how could anyone else compare them? Faith enables us to see with the eyes of heaven to discern these things.

So let's run the race with our eyes on the prize, refusing to concern ourselves with the here and now, for the prize will be worth it all.

Let this be your heart's cry Mighty Warrior:

"So we're not to give up! Even though on the outside it often looks like things are falling apart, on the inside, where God is creating something brand new, and not a day goes by that He does not pour out His grace. Those hard times are small potatoes compared to the coming good times—the lavish celebration prepared for us. There's far more here than meets the eye. The things we see now are here today, gone tomorrow. But the things we can't see now will last forever." (See 2 Corinthians 4:16-18, MSG.)

Steve Porter

The Threshing Floor

"Thou hast caused men <u>to ride over our heads</u>; we went through fire and through water: but thou broughtest us out into <u>a wealthy place</u>."
(Psalms 66:12)

My Precious Child,

Carefully consider these words: **"Unless a grain of wheat is buried in the ground, dead to the world, it is never any more than a grain of wheat. But if it is buried, it sprouts and reproduces itself many times over."** (John 12:24)

My child, you are exactly like one grain of wheat, a single seed. And you come to maturity by dying to yourself and coming alive to Me. This kind of obedience will reproduce, impacting the lives of others in ways you can't yet imagine. I want to greatly multiply your past effectiveness, kingdom impact, and spiritual maturity, but that can only happen as you are changed into My likeness and take on My character.

Consider the process of harvesting grain. When grain is ready for harvest, it is cut with a flint sickle, and the grain is bound into sheaves. From there, the grain is transported to the threshing floor.

At times, I will put you through a process much like the threshing of wheat. You may feel as if you have been cut down and set aside just like that sheaf of wheat. However, let me reassure you that this process transforms you into a useful seed that I can use to feed the spiritual needs of a lost and dying world. And lest you believe otherwise, let me say that, unless this occurs, you will be of no use left in the fields to rot where you are, eventually withering away.

When you're sent to the threshing floor, it's natural to panic, for you're being taken to an unfamiliar place, and the unknown looms large before you. But if you're convinced of My tender love and My plan for your welfare, you can rest in Me, knowing the outcome will be amazing.

This process may seem cruel from your human perspective, but it transforms you so that you see with heaven's eyes, and I can refine you into a pure, clear reflection of Myself. At times it will mean being hurt if that's what it takes to refine you. **("Thou has caused men to ride over our heads.")** I know that those times aren't easy, but I will be with you there, comforting you and reminding you of my steadfast love, until you get to that **"wealthy place."**

After all the impurities are exposed I will send My Holy Spirit to convict you so that you bow to My will and yearn for Me to transform you.

And finally, I fine tune your spirit to be responsive to My still, small voice, so that you run when I call. I fill you with compassion, giving you a heart like Mine, so that your countenance is changed, and people can see Me in you. It is on the threshing floor where your life is transformed.

Working in harmony with me I will use you, empower you, to go feed the spiritually hungry. Will you go?

Honey in the Carcass

"Later, when he returned to Timnah for the wedding, he turned off the path to look at the carcass of the lion. And he found that a swarm of bees had made some honey in the carcass."
(Judges 14:8, NLT)

My Precious Child,

Even as Samson walked a road toward Timnah and a young lion sprang toward him and roared, yet my spirit came upon him with such force that Samson tore the lion apart with his bare hands; he had no weapon other than My power.

In the same way I was with Samson I will also be with you as you face the lions of life! They will attempt to terrorize and destroy you as if you were just a goat or a lamb. They roar and send waves of fear that paralyze my children. Yet the same power that caused Samson to rip apart the lion with his bare hands also dwells in you! I live within you, so stir up that anointing and refuse to allow the enemy to cripple you another moment.

The enemy of your soul, like a roaring lion, seeks to devour My children, yet I am the Lion of Judah! When I roar all others must bow before My great power. Samson faced the lion and conquered it and so will you. After some time had passed he once again passed the place where he had fought the lion, and saw that only its carcass remained. Its flesh had been devoured so only the skeleton survived.

My child, I want you to see My hand at work here. Your past contains the carcass of the lion that is dead and can no longer hurt you! All that remains is the carcass of painful defeats of your past. The young lion that once brought fear and intimidation now lies dead at your feet. The power of the Holy Spirit has brought the victory. Not even your failures can hurt you anymore unless you believe and speak otherwise to empower them.

Once you repent of past failures and bad choices, they have no power to hinder you or abort your destiny. For the righteous may fall but they should choose to stand and fight once again. The enemy, however, will try to tear you down with words of failure, discouragement and weariness, telling you that you will never be victorious, but put him in his place with words of faith that agree with My Word, and he will flee in terror at My name. I have given you power and authority over everything the devil can throw at you, but many of My children remain victimized because they fail to believe Me and act accordingly in faith to thwart the evil plans of the enemy.

When you choose to agree with My Will and My Word, I render harmless the young lions that attempt to destroy your purpose and destiny. I will fight for you as you stand in unity with My power and refuse to doubt. I will even place something sweet within that old carcass for you. Just as Samson found a swarm of bees with honey in the skeleton of that lion, I am going to bring something sweet into your life from even the dead places.

I will bring good even from life's fiercest battles. Don't worry about fighting the bees, for they are going to bring something productive into your life. I can even turn your failures into something sweet, so don't be afraid to pass those skeletons on the road of life and see clearly the lessons I am teaching you. I will give the revelation, the goodness, and even the honey in order to mature you. Reach in and sweep out the honey from the dead places in your life.

The enemy will try to declare that you are defenseless and useless to My kingdom, but I say otherwise, so believe what I say. If you have a skeleton in your closet, repent and let me disarm the enemy with that sweet spirit of repentance, forgiveness and restoration. The only thing that matters is what I declare. Perhaps you have been discouraged and despairing after listening to the lies of the enemy and have walked great distances to avoid looking at the carcasses in your life. Then hear this—there's honey in that carcass.

Once you've repented I will turn that carcass into a thing of beauty that I will use to draw others to Me, as you tell of the great things the Lord has done on your behalf. Give those dead things to Me, and I will turn them into honey for you. Watch and see the salvation of your God!

Your Identity is Found in Me

"He has identified us as his own by placing the Holy Spirit in our hearts."
(2 Corinthians 1:22a, NLT)

My Precious Child,

Do not let Satan diminish or discourage you! He's hard at work in the earth today distorting the images in my children's minds regarding their identity in Me. My deepest desire is for your faith to grow stronger and more mature, but that cannot happen until you see yourself through My eyes. You must completely cast down any image of yourself that does not agree with My Word.

You've let others put you in a box by speaking limits into your life, when I intend for you to soar. My analysis is not based on human understanding, but rather I see you through the eyes of faith—knowing what you're capable of doing by the power of the Holy Spirit. Others may speak death to My plan for you, but I will have the final word!

You must embark on the journey of faith, believing how

much your heavenly Father treasures you and how pleased He is to have created you. Do you know that I stand over you and sing a song of rejoicing over the day you were born? Recall that word picture when you struggle to believe what I say.

My Word teaches that I love you perfectly—unconditionally. My perfect love is not based on your performance; it is who I am, and the fact is that I can be no other way (see 1 John 4:8). I will always love you, but often you can't receive my love because of guilt over your past. And while I never wink at sin, and My grace is never a license to rebel, I want you to know who I created you to be—to "sing like no one's listening, love like you've never been hurt, dance like nobody's watching, and live like it's heaven on earth." (Mark Twain) But that's only possible if you choose to be deaf to every other voice but Mine.

Don't go by your feelings, for they are fickle and deceptive, changing like the direction of the wind. Don't measure yourself by the situations you encounter, because they don't determine your success or failure. Stop measuring your success by who you know, how much you earn, where you live, or what you drive, rather remember the times you were down in the dumps and I was faithful to lift you up and set your feet on high places, making you victorious. Put your confidence in Me, knowing that I have never failed you, and I never will.

I am the one who defines you, and I say that you cannot fail as long as you're attached to the Vine.

If you're unsure of your identity, you're vulnerable to those who want to tear you down. But the truth is that you are who I say you are, and you can do what I say you can do. No one else has a vote in the matter.

The identity issue must be addressed in order to live the deeper abundant life, leaving the past behind. When you identify with Me, I put My power at your fingertips, so that nothing shall be impossible for you. I created you exactly the way you are; I am pleased and delighted with you, so live as if it is so.

I don't want you to live in exhaustion, frustrated and miserable with no sense of value, so look for your identity in Me alone. Let My Word be the basis for your confidence. Remember, Colossians 1:27 that says, **"The kingdom of God is within you."** Continually reinforce the truth, and your outlook will be transformed by the renewing of your mind.

Psalm 139:14 tells us we are fearfully and wonderfully made. Romans 8:35 says that nothing can separate you from My love. So no longer allow the enemy to steal your identity. You are My masterpiece, so choose now to believe it. Perhaps you've heard the phrase, "God said it, so that settles it." Let that be your motto, and see miracles happen. Only believe!

He Leads Me Beside Still Waters

In the Wilderness

"Who is this that cometh out of the wilderness like pillars of smoke,

perfumed with myrrh and frankincense, with all powders of the merchant?"
(Song of Solomon 3:6)

"Who is this that cometh up from the wilderness, leaning upon her beloved?"
(Song of Solomon 8:5a)

My Precious Child,

It is in the wilderness that I will seek to add a new dimension to you. I will broaden your Christian experience. I will deepen your relationship with Me and transform you into My image. To put it another way, Hosea 2:14 says: **«Therefore, behold, I will allure her and bring her into the wilderness and speak tenderly unto her.»** At this place I will separate you for Myself, and make you ready for your destiny. I will give you a deep longing for Me so that you seek My presence with all that is in you, in response to My great love. And beyond the wilderness you will find a special place of blessing, where you will be glad and rejoice that you have been there. For a time you may weep in the wilderness, but I will comfort you and give you a new and joyful song.

The wilderness is My perfume shop where the perfume of My presence will saturate you as you take upon yourself my life and character, becoming ever more like Me in character and desires. My perfume is not an outer adornment, but an inner fragrance that identifies with Me. Itɔs the perfume of My presence that is found only in one place—the place of intimacy with Me.

When the time in that place has ended I, your bridegroom. will bring out you, My bride, and present you to the world, beautiful, radiant and scented with the fragrance of My love. At that point, we will be inseparable, because you will lean on and depend on Me for your very breath, your very being. And even if the whole lot comes against us, nothing will separate us from one another. In fact, I will say to you, «Come away with Me. Lean on Me, and we will go out to the wilderness together.» In the end, you will be the envy of your friends (the daughters of Jerusalem) who will smell the sweet fragrance and want what you have.

If you draw near to Me, and refuse to stray, I will bless and exalt you. I will give you an ever-increasing revelation of Myself. I will come for you, and offer you My arm for support, along with My endless strength and endurance, and bring you out smelling incredibly beautiful, like Me, and your beauty will be the envy of everyone who sees you. It is in this place that a new thing, a brand new dimension, will be added unto you, and you and I will be as one...

Steve Porter

Finding Rest in the Wilderness

"But for many of them God was not pleased; for they were overthrown in the wilderness."
(1 Corinthians 10:5)

My Precious Child,

I know that, at times, you feel as if you've just come out of one trial when you face another one. This is how the children of Israel felt when they journeyed out of the wilderness of Sinai and into the wilderness of Paran.

'So the Israelites set out from the wilderness of Sinai and traveled on from place to place until the cloud stopped in the wilderness of Paran.' (Numbers 10:12)

Notice that I led them by a cloud that hovered over them, filled with My glorious manifest presence.

I can hear you saying that you don't understand why I would lead you right from one test into another. You may feel that loss of direction or not know what to do. Many times you inquire of others, asking them why, but I am the only source of answers for you.

in 2 Corinthians 11:26 Paul said this about the wilderness experience:

"**In** journeying often, **in** perils of waters, **in** perils of robbers, **in** perils by **mine own countrymen, in** perils by the heathen, **in** perils in the city, <u>in perils in the wilderness</u>, **in** perils in the sea, **in** perils among false brethren." (2 Corinthians 11:26)

He faced what seemed like continual defeat, yet I was at work, leading him through each trial. He was not defeated in the wilderness, but, in fact, was made stronger and chose to run his race to the very end. **He** kept pursuing the goal to win the high calling of knowing Me intimately.

An emotional high will not see you through such times of testing; only rock solid faith firmly anchored in Me will see you through. Let your heart and mind be firmly fixed on my Word, so that its roots go deep and your confidence doesn't fail in times of testing. Do not lose hope; put your faith in Me and I will also lead you through to victory. I want you to know Me so well that you don't give in to unbelief and confusion.

'So I was angry with them, and I said, "Their hearts always turn away from me. They refuse to do what I tell them." So in my anger I took an oath: "They will never enter my place of rest." Be careful then, dear brothers and sister. Make sure that your own hearts are not evil and unbelieving, turning you away from the living God.' (Hebrews 3:10-12)

There will be times when you don't understand My ways and you will also be tempted to walk away in fear. Stand fast and place your trust in Me and discover my divine rest. Your enemy would love to discourage you and cause you to walk away from Me, so you miss your divine purpose. In the end, though, the wilderness is dangerous, it is the place where you learn to trust Me as never before, and where you begin to look just like Me.

No matter how dead or dry you feel, or how far I seem to be from you, My presence is always there. I will be your strong tower and My presence will go with you, if you feel it or not, as I lead you to your promised land. And once you can trust Me, and let nothing rock your boat, I will lead you from glory to glory.

Apple of My Eye

"Do you not know that your help cometh from the Lord?"
(Psalms 121:2)

My Precious Child,

You may not be aware of it, but I am concerned even with the mundane details of your life. I care about each and every one. Even as the adrenaline flows in the physical, as you reach up to Me I will give you a supernatural flow of My Spirit, and you will receive My divine strength and power to make it through every challenge.

Cast your cares upon Me even now. What is weighing you down? Clearly the anxieties of life have stolen your joy so that you're consumed with fear and worry. But it doesn't have to be that way!

Do you recall the Scripture in John 16:33 that says, **'These things I have spoken unto you, that in me ye might have peace. In the world ye shall have tribulation, but be of good cheer; I have overcome the world.'**

Consider what I have done for you. I have given you salvation, taking all your sins upon My body, so that you could go free. I have set you in a high place, where no evil will befall you, nor shall any plague come near your dwelling. I have written your name in the Lamb's Book of Life, and no one can take you out of the safety of My hand. (Rev. 21:27) I also have a Book of Remembrance where I have recorded your every act of faithfulness, and I never forget even one of them. (Malachi 3:15) Did you get that? I know you intimately, and love you dearly.

In Psalms 56:8 My Word records that I have bottled every tear you shed—yes, I collect them all, because each one is precious to Me. In Matthew 10:30 I wrote that I keep track of the number of hairs on your head, and in Isaiah 49:16 it says that "your image" is engraved in the palm of My mighty hand! Don't forget that I also declare in Zechariah 2:8 that you are the apple of My eye, the center of my attention. Can you see, My child, how important you are to Me?

More precious promises: I will keep and guard you with My eye upon you. (Ps. 17:8)

Even when you find yourself in frightening situations I will be there to protect you. Deut. 32:9-10: '**For the people of Israel belong to the Lord; Jacob and his special possession. He found them in a desert land, in an empty, howling wasteland. He surrounded them and watched over them; he guarded them as he would guard his own eyes.**'

I will protect you. You are special to Me. I encircle you with My unfailing love. When you are in danger or need I will empower you with faith and wrap you in a warm blanket of My comforting presence. I will dispatch hosts of ministering, warring, guardian angels to surround you. I will send my Holy Spirit to comfort you. You are my delight, the very apple of my eye. Reach for Me even now, for I am here waiting to hold you close...

I Never Sleep

"Then he returned to his disciples and found them sleeping. "Could you men not keep watch with me for one hour?"
(Matthew 26:40)

My Precious Child,

My heart was heavy with grief when I knelt in the garden that night. I was crushed and overwhelmed, sweating drops of blood from the reality of the cross I would need to face the following day. I pleaded with My disciples to stay awake to support Me in prayer, but I carried this burden alone—they all slept as I knelt there with no one but God to encourage and comfort Me.

Three times I pleaded with them to pray with Me, but each time I found them curled up sleeping, unmoved by the urgency of the hour. I wept, asking My Father for this cup to pass, yet I submitted My will to His as I reached out to Him. During that terrible time I longed for My disciples to surround Me with love and support, yet they slept on, unaware of the trials I would endure, until it was too late.

I know what it's like to wrestle with a burden alone without support, but, My precious one, I want you to know you're never alone, for I am with you always, even during your darkest night. I do not slumber or sleep, I'm aware of every burden you carry and I will never leave you or forsake you.

Can you hear what I'm saying? I never sleep where you're concerned. I'm aware of every burden you carry, so make your requests known to Me and I will answer you.

When you feel as if heaven is silent and sleeping, this is when things are most active behind the scenes. I am up and about, moving and rearranging things, and preparing your circumstances for your greater good! As soon as you release your burden at My feet I am already picking it up and making a way of escape for you.

Put your faith in Me—trust in My words with all your heart, take confidence in My never-ending supply of support and sustaining grace. I will lift you up. I will carry you. I will see you through. In fact, I am planning the details of your victory parade right now! You will make it through, because I never sleep. Look to the hills, for your help comes from Me!

My child it is written:

> **"He will not let you be defeated.**
>
> **He who guards you never sleeps.**
>
> [4] **He who guards Israel**

> never rests or sleeps.
>
> [5] **The Lord guards you.**
>
> **The Lord is the shade that protects you from the sun.**
>
> [6] **The sun cannot hurt you during the day,**
>
> **and the moon cannot hurt you at night.**
>
> [7] **The Lord will protect you from all dangers;**
>
> **he will guard your life.**
>
> [8] **The Lord will guard you as you come and go,**
>
> **both now and forever."**
>
> (Psalms 121:3-8, NCV)

I AM your Provider, your Protector, and your Victory. If you'll release your burdens to Me with great expectations, I will miraculously make a way. So trust Me now, as never before, and see the salvation of your God!

Can I Call You Friend?

"No longer do I call you servants, for a servant does not know what his master is doing; but I have called you friends..." (John 15:15a)

My Precious Child,

Do not let your heart be troubled or discouraged, for I am nearer to you than at any time in the past. I am bringing you into a place of stability and consistency where you will not be moved or overcome. I will hold you firmly in My righteous right hand regardless of what you are feeling. You do not need to always see My face to know that I am near. Believe My Word that says I never leave or forsake you. In fact, you can reach for My hand by faith in moments when you feel that I am far away. Embrace Me with all your heart, and let Me give you a personal revelation of who I Am. Push aside the distractions of the world, and follow hard after Me. I Am always anticipating your return to our secret place.

Did you know that not all My servants are actually close friends? Some are merely doing their duty, spending time with Me out of obligation, when what I really want is intimacy, where I can tell you My secrets and My plans, talking with you about anything and everything. I can›t do that with servants, but I can do that with friends. Will you be My friend, and come into the secret place where we can just be ourselves and talk? Will you linger awhile and not be in a hurry to leave? I long for those moments... I›m lonely for your company. Where are you, My dove?

Come Away with Me

"My beloved is like a roe or a young hart; behold, he standeth behind our wall, he looketh forth at the windows, shewing himself through the lattice."
(Song of Solomon 2:9)

My Precious Child,

I, the Lord, stand outside the wall looking through the window. I patiently wait for you, calling out softly, «Rise up, My darling! Come away with Me, My fair one!» Then I wait for your response. Will you agree to «come away»? Will you leave the distractions of the world and come away? Will you set aside your normal routine—your to-do list—and sit with Me awhile?

I show Myself to you, letting you know I am here. I look through the window, slowly revealing My presence in hopes you will notice Me. Will you? Or do you sit alone, content with the blessings I›ve provided, while I, the Lord of glory, wait, alone and lonely for your company? As hard as it is to believe, I long for your company, for intimacy with you. I want you to know you have a higher purpose, to go deeper and bask in My presence, in My arms, where you can finally rest and find true contentment, totally secure in who you are.

As your heavenly Bridegroom, I'm not content to simply let you hear stories about My manifest presence. I want you to draw near and have fellowship with Me in the secret place. I long to share the reality of My manifest presence with you, for it is there that I will awaken your desires for more of Me and reveal to you the deep things of the Spirit.

The word 'manifest' means to make visible to one of your five senses. Within that sacred precinct are the very chambers where you can enter the place I dwell and sit with Me awhile. I actually hesitate to open Myself up and make Myself known, because I have been repeatedly wounded by those who take lightly My mighty presence and power. As a result I am cautious when approaching those I seek, to discover whether they really want Me, or simply say the words.

Do you really relate to Me only because of My blessing, but keep your distance, refusing to come any closer? Don't be afraid of that provision, because it's just a doorway leading to the secret place where you can meet Me face to face and have a personal visitation from a very personal Christ.

Will you look over and see Me standing alone? Will you keep Me standing there or bid Me come and sit with you awhile? For it's only in sweet, intimate fellowship that I reveal Myself to you. I don't want you to be content to hear the stories; I want you to discover Me for yourself.

Walking with Me requires transparency, where you are unguarded, unafraid, and free of pretense, free to be yourself, even when we just share the details of our day. Beloved, I know the number of hairs on your head; how much more do I care about the little things in your life? Such transparency will surprise you, and make you want more, because I fill up the empty places you've been trying to fill on your own for years.

I don't want you to put on airs or speak memorized or complex prayers. I take great delight in simple conversations with you, being friends and sharing hearts, talking face to face. This happens when you are honest with Me, simply sharing your heart, because that is the place where miracles start. I'm waiting...

Running After Me

"Draw me, we will run after thee: the king hath brought me into his chambers."
(Song of Solomon 1:4a)

My Precious Child,

I am wooing you by My spirit into a place of rest found only in My presence. I have placed inside you a tugging on your heart, a deep spiritual yearning that only I can satisfy—a longing that nothing else can fill.

Many are content to seek only what I can give, with no desire to spend time with Me. Others come to Me only for their needs and wants, and, although I desire to meet your needs, I am drawing you beyond that place, straight to My heart. I want you to move beyond My hands into My arms where I will embrace you and our hearts will become one. At the place where we move in unity, I will use you to be My hands extended to a lost and dying world. Will you answer the call?

When I hear you pray, "Draw me, Lord," you open the door to the secret place found in My presence, a place where miracles happen, and I reveal Myself to you in ways you could never discover anywhere else. I want nothing more than to increase that deep longing inside you—to take you deeper, showing you My very heart. Will you cry out for more, and let your heart yearn after Me?

As I am increasing your desire for Me, you will feel a deep desire to run after Me as never before, in devoted pursuit. (We will run after thee.) In the process you will be set apart for Me alone. I will wash and purify your heart and mind, so that they belong to only Me. Old things will pass away and, behold, all things will become new as you run after Me with all your heart. Even old dead branches will be pruned away, so that you will bear much beautiful fruit.

Your obedience causes Me to take action... I will take you into My chambers, that special place of intimacy, that safe place of refuge where I will strengthen, mature and instruct you. In that place I can reveal Myself to you in a personal way. Can you hear Me wooing you to come deeper? Will you pursue Me with all your heart?

My child, cry out to Me with a spiritual hunger, a yearning to see My face. Let Me increase your desperation for Me alone. Run after Me, and accept nothing less, for I will open My heart to you. Come and abide in Me. Seek Me and dwell in my chambers—that special place of rest and peace.

I want to be closer to you, for you to know My ways and behold My beauty. My heart leaps every time you run after Me. I am waiting for you! Will you come that I may show My face to you—My deepest secrets?

Steve Porter

Keeping Me Company

*"Open to me, my darling, my treasure, my lovely dove,
he said, for I have been out in the night.
My head is soaked with dew, my hair with the wetness
of the night."
(Song of Solomon 5:2b, NLT)*

My Precious Child,

As your Bridegroom I seek you in the dark night hours, to see if you're awake. I go out and come to you, knocking at your door to see if you'll let Me in, out of the cold night air. I long to be with you, so we can talk and share secrets, but often you're already sleeping, without a care for Me, not knowing I'm out here waiting for you to let Me come in. Or do you know I'm waiting? Perhaps you just don't care. You already have the gifts of My hands, so maybe you don't need Me at all. I shake My head and turn away, searching for a house with the light on, waiting for Me to come. I wipe away tears, missing you, wishing you were the one.

I long to come in out of the cold, to sit by your nice warm

fire and feel the warmth of your friendship, your smile and the touch of your hand. I yearn for someone to keep Me company in the quietness of the night. Will you be one of those I call on, who rises to turn on the light?

Oh, I know the day hours work best for you, that you're tired after your long days, but don't you know I can give you more rest as we visit the hours away? How much do you love Me, My beloved, enough to give up your sleep? Enough to interrupt your slumber when I call at the midnight so deep? I want you to know Me, to love Me, to treasure Me more than the air, I want you to yearn for My presence, to want Me to come to you there. The choice is yours...

Let this be your response: Lord, I refuse to allow You to stand out in the cold and for your head to collect the dew of the night. I will meet You in our secret place any time You call. When You announce your presence, I will open the door and invite You inside, my friend and dearest Lord.

Come, Lord Jesus...

Seasons of Life

"And of the children of Issachar, which were men that had understanding of the times, to know what Israel ought to do."
(1 Chronicles 12:32a)

My Precious Child,

Some seasons pass quickly, while others stay longer than they should, and some over-stay their welcome. Just as it occurs in the natural, you will also experience spiritual seasons of winter, spring, summer, and fall in practically every aspect of your life. It could be in your marriage, job, ministry, money, or even in your spiritual development.

Consider the Sons of Issachar who had spiritual discernment regarding the times and seasons as well as certain choices that needed to be made in a timely manner. I enabled them to recognize the seasons and follow My will, to victory.

The coming of winter ushers in colder weather and fewer daylight hours that can lead you to believe that life is bleak and desolate. As with so many things in life, your attitude toward this special time of year is based on your thoughts and perceptions. Now it's time to see things with the eyes of heaven. Winter is a wonderful time of year to rest, relax, and recharge, allowing you to enjoy the fruits of your labor from the previous year. It's a time to reflect on past achievements, contemplate previous mistakes, and hear My voice as you plan for the future.

Yet spring is only a few short months away, the perfect time to plant new seeds of opportunity, to carry out plans we envisioned during the preceding dark winter months. You will need to focus your mental, physical, and spiritual energies on the spring so that you may till the once-frozen winter soil of your creative vision before planting your next crop of ideas and fertilizing them with prayer.

Then comes summer. The seeds of opportunity have already been planted, but the work has only just begun. This is the time of year that requires consistent nurturing of your newly planted dreams and hopes. Your ideas are always at risk of being squelched by the harsh climate of life's circumstances, and the summertime is when you need to really focus on weeding and watering to reap the best rewards. In the summer, you'll begin to see the first sprouts of evidence that all your hard work and careful planning are beginning to pay off.

Then comes autumn, ripe with the fruit of your efforts, and ready for picking. This is a time of gratitude and thanksgiving, and a time to store your harvest for the coming year. You can now see the benefit of all your hard work from previous seasons, carefully maximizing their benefits over the long term.

Without the ability to correctly discern the proper seasons and My intentions for each one, you can often become confused and disheartened. You may be inclined to harvest your opportunities in the winter instead of in autumn, or you may want to plant new ideas and creative opportunities during the wrong seasons. With discernment, you're better able to hear My Word, and follow My lead during those ever-changing seasons of life.

From now on, it's vital to prophetically discern the times and the seasons that I have you in, in order to move with the Holy Spirit into the place I have for you. Often you allow the fear of change to bring confusion and stress into your life; you begin to question Me and frustration sets in. I desire for you to transition into new seasons without feeling panic and hopelessness.

I realize that it's not easy to move from one season to another. I never promised you it would always be easy, but I did promise that I would be with you through every transition. In fact, I'll be nearby, holding you close, and encouraging you ahead. The key to moving from season to season is to have discernment and know that I'm moving you forward.

Don't be afraid to ask the Holy Spirit when you notice things begin to rumble and shake in your life. Remember the petitions you prayed in previous seasons; dig out the prophetic words I've given you in the past and focus on those promises. This will bring clarity to distinguish between My work and the work of the enemy. Stay close to My heart because things are not always as they seem, especially in the face of great disappointment.

Once you know that I'm ushering you into a fresh new season, quickly align your will with Mine. Surrender your agenda to Me, and be very sensitive to My leadings. Don't resist a change in seasons, but ask Me for the grace to rise to the occasion and fulfill your destiny. Stay humble and obedient to My perfect will.

No matter what season you're in, be encouraged, for I am the Lord, and I will bring you through all the changes, into your season of harvest! The seasons may change; the winds will blow, but I am the God of all seasons! (Gal. 6:9)

Yet... I will Rejoice

"Though the fig tree does not bud and there are no grapes on the vines, though the olive crop fails and the fields produce no food, though there are no sheep in the pen and no cattle in the stalls,
18 yet I will rejoice in the Lord, I will be joyful in God my savior."
(Habakkuk 3:17-18)

My Precious Child,

There will be seasons where you may feel that all is lost—that this is the last straw and that the contrary winds blow, bringing nothing but barrenness and famine. Negativity preoccupies your thoughts and you find no peace anywhere.

These contrary winds come as all manner of trials, tests, struggles, and difficulties. It is written **'that people are born for trouble as readily as sparks fly up from a fire.'** (Job 5:7) Because of man's fallen state, trouble will continue until I come on that glorious day of My return.

In this life you will face seasons of difficulty, for I never promised that you wouldn't face a storm, but I have promised to see you though every storm! I am the Prince of Peace who never leaves you alone. I long to gather you up in my arms and protect you as a mother hen gathers up her chicks and hovers over them when danger comes. You are safe under My shadow; My abiding presence is with you always, even to the ends of the earth.

You can rejoice in Me, your Savior, knowing I carry you in the palms of my hands. Your name is etched on my heart, and your face is ever before Me. Stay the course, and trust me no matter what the fig trees does or how the vine flourishes. I am the Lord of the fig tree, and I am the Lord of the vine!

Rejoice in Me during the storms with absolute expectation and hope. Put your confidence in Me and look not with natural vision or ordinary reasoning. I declare over you right now, My child, that you are coming into a new season! Because:

8"My thoughts are nothing like your thoughts," says the LORD.

"And my ways are far beyond anything you could imagine.

9For just as the heavens are higher than the earth,

so my ways are higher than your ways

and my thoughts higher than your thoughts.

10"The rain and snow come down from the heavens

and stay on the ground to water the earth.

They cause the grain to grow,

producing seed for the farmer

and bread for the hungry.

11It is the same with my word.

I send it out, and it always produces fruit.

It will accomplish all I want it to,

and it will prosper everywhere I send it.

12You will live in joy and peace.

The mountains and hills will burst into song,

and the trees of the field will clap their hands!

13Where once there were thorns, cypress trees will grow.

Where nettles grew, myrtles will sprout up.

These events will bring great honor to the LORD's name;

they will be an everlasting sign of his power and love."

(Isaiah 55 8-13)

Be encouraged, knowing that I have already anticipated what you need. I have already gone before you to the place that looks impossible, and I have made provision for you that you can't even imagine. Choose to believe this with the eyes of faith, refusing to doubt, and watch the salvation of your Mighty God!

Dear Heavenly Father, In all of our difficulty we know that You are there. We choose to put our trust in You no matter what we see with our natural eyes. Continue to reveal yourself to us personally during those times. Thank You, Father, for bringing us this far in our lives. We have gone too far to quit now for You will never, ever let us go!

In Jesus' name. Amen....

Steve Porter

Savor What Really Matters

*"You do not know what happens tomorrow.
For what is your life? It is even a vapor that appears
for a little time and then vanishes away."
(James 4:14)*

My Precious Child,

Your journey toward Death's door actually begins at the moment of your birth, progressing at a steady, unwavering pace towards a final destination that seems all so distant in your earliest years of childhood. As you approach closer and closer, year after year, your previously infantile denial begins to slowly turn to feelings of mortality until you are anxiously awaiting My Holy Presence who will be waiting for you on the other side. Some find out when it's too late, deep in sickness they become attentive to Death sitting at their bedside.

Did I not say that the life I have given you is short? It's like a vapor or a puff of smoke that you only see for a short time before it disappears! What a tiny portion is allotted to man to prepare for eternity.

Though it may seem long at times, life really doesn't last long. Keeping this revelation close to your heart allows you to see from an eternal perspective. Eternity is long—much like trying to count all the grains of sand—your years will number further than any man can possibly count. In fact, you will live forever. But will you love Me to the end of time? Will you steward the time I've given you until we meet face to face?

I love you with an everlasting love, and you prove your love for Me here on Earth. Know this: in less than the time it takes to blink, you'll exit this life. Time is precious, and life is fragile. And because every minute counts, I'm asking you to be a faithful steward of every breath. Things will quickly pass away so I want you to hold on to what will stand the test of time, redeeming the time because the days are evil.

'Make the most of every opportunity in these evil days.' (Ephesians 5:16)

Savor what really matters in the here and now. Each moment you savor in My presence is not time wasted but wisely invested, because in those moments together I will pour into you wisdom, directing your steps to move in My will to change the world. What you gain in the Spirit will last for all eternity. Therefore, set yourself apart to rest in My presence, for what you now sow to the Spirit you will reap in the life to come.

For as the wise virgins prepared for My coming by keeping oil in their lamps so you will be prepared for the marriage supper of the Lamb by filling yourself with the oil of My presence. I'm coming for a bride who's set herself apart and has been preparing herself especially for Me. The foolish virgins slept and did not yearn for my appearing, so today they sleep while many others are content in their apathy, because they don't see with an eternal perspective. I want every moment of your life here on Earth to count for something. Paul said, "I will have reason to glory because I did not run in vain, nor toil in vain."

"Hold firm to the word of life; then, on the day of Christ's return, I will be proud that I did not run the race in vain and that my work was not useless." (Philippians 2:16)

Do not run the race of life in vain, savor what really matters. It is required of stewards that they be found trustworthy.

"Now, a person who is put in charge as a manager must be faithful." (1 Corinthians 4:2)

Can I trust you with the time I've given you? Live with eternity's values in view, with your eye on the goal. Redeem the time, savor what really matters, and sow to the Spirit. Rest in My presence, and stir up the passion for My imminent return, for soon you will stand before Me, content and blessed, knowing you were a faithful steward.

He Leads Me Beside Still Waters

Let Your Light so Shine

"Let your light so shine before men, that they may see your good works, and glorify your Father which is in heaven."
(Matthew 5:16)

My Precious Child,

I have called you **'for such a time as this.'** (Esther 4:14) Therefore do not sleep, as do others; but rather watch and be sober! Sadly, great darkness has fallen upon the earth and many today have fallen asleep and allowed their light to grow dim. I am calling you to **be** the light that invades that darkness and brings a fresh revelation of My glory and splendor to all of mankind.

Who would light a lamp and then cover it up? They would light the lamp and place it in a noticeable place so that others can find their way. Even so, you as my child must be that light to the world, so hold it up high that they may find Me when they see you.

I want the way of redemption to become clearly visible to even those who choose to walk in darkness. I want you to be so passionate, so earnest, so sincere, so courageous, so diligent, and so full of my presence that others will discover Me in your face. Did I not say that **"The path of the just is as a shining light?"** (Prov. 4:18)

I want your "light (to) break forth as the morning" (Is. 58:8) so that you "walk worthy of your calling." (Eph. 4:1, 1 Thess. 2:12) Live your lives in such holiness that I can't help but be pleased and blessed, for I called you to be part of ushering in My glorious kingdom. Don't give anyone a reason to criticize or blame you, but be innocent, holy children of God, and let your light so shine that a crooked and perverse generation may see it and glorify your Father which is in heaven.

Go out into the world uncorrupted, a breath of fresh air in this squalid and polluted society. Provide people with a glimpse of good living and of the living God. Carry the light-giving Message into the night... (See Phil. 2:15, MSG)

My children should be distinctly different from the world. The darker the night, the brighter the light should shine through you. Keep yourselves blameless and pure, so that others will see and be convicted, saving their very souls in the process. You are to be like a lighthouse, whose dazzling light illumines even the darkest stormy night, to warn others of the dangers of hell, and lead them safely home.

And not only should your conversation be holy and honorable, but the life you live should shout that I live in you, for your life speaks louder than any sermon. Stir up the passion inside you for Me, and refuse to compromise or to be a stumbling block to the weak, bringing shame to My name.

If you have fallen short is this area, it's not too late to start over, for I am the God of the second chance—the fresh start. Bow in repentance at the foot of the cross, and find redemption in My nail scarred hands. I will replace your garment of shame for a robe of righteousness through My shed blood.

"Walk in a manner worthy of the calling with which you have been called."

(Ephesians 4:1) **"For you are a chosen generation, a royal priesthood, an holy nation."** (1 Peter 2:9) Be the light; invade the darkness, and let your life be the lighthouse that will guide My children home.

The God of the Turn Around

"Every valley [in your life] shall be exalted...the crooked places [in your life] shall be made straight... and the rough places [in your life] smooth. The glory of the Lord shall be revealed [to you]...for the mouth of the Lord has spoken" (Isaiah 40:4-5)

My Precious Child,

I am the God of the turnaround! For some time now you have been asking Me when things are going to turn around—when the winds of change are going to start blowing, when the winds of favor will head your way. Well, the time is now, and I'm going to begin to restore everything that the locust has eaten!

It's time for your turnaround. Did I not make a pathway for My people through the Red Sea? Did I not provide water from a rock to give refreshment? Did I not send manna and quail to feed My people? Did I not give direction by a cloud during the day and a pillar of fire during the night to lead them?

If I did that for My people then don't I care just as much about you? Can I not bring order from your chaos or refreshment from the dry places in your life? Can I not resurrect even the dead things?

I can change the heart of your stubborn boss, contentious spouse, or rebellious child. In a moment I can transform your finances and restore your broken relationships. And I can give you a new ministry far more effective than the last one.

I'm about to shatter anything that's holding you back or keeping you down. My Holy Spirit is about to pay you a visit with great power, strength, grace and anointing, giving you new clarity and divine wisdom. Are you ready?

I declare over you that the enemy must release his grip on your marriage, health, and finances. He must release your family and cannot abort your purpose and destiny. The enemy's tactics and lies are being exposed and destroyed in My name.

I am the God of the turnaround! I will heal your disappointments. I will heal your pain. I will heal your brokenness and turn your mess into a message to bring Me honor.

'For I know the plans I have for you," says the Lord. "They are plans for good and not for disaster, to give you a future and a hope.' (Jeremiah 29:11)

This is not a time to fold your hands and fall asleep. It's a time to decree and declare that you have victory through

Me. So ask Me today for your turnaround.

I'm releasing favor over you. I'm restoring your honor and giving you a fresh mandate from heaven. I am ready to arise and scatter your enemies. (Psalms 68:1)

But you need to rise up. Lift your holy hands to Me and worship My face. Declare that I am your healer, your restorer, your provider and your peace. I am the God of the turnaround, and I will fulfill my promises over your life. You may be delayed but you will not be denied.

When I restore all, I want you to remember your Source. Lean upon Me always, and never lose sight of what it means to walk in true humility and dependence. I am your God, and I will increase you once again. Only walk humbly before Me, and give Me the glory. More than anything else, I yearn for time with you. So never lose sight of that.

I declare over you even now:

'Every valley [in your life] shall be exalted...the crooked places [in your life] shall be made straight... and the rough places [in your life] smooth. The glory of the Lord shall be revealed [to you]...for the mouth of the Lord has spoken.' (Isaiah 40:4-5)

My desire for you will always prevail, because I am the God of turnaround!

He Leads Me Beside Still Waters

In Remembrance

"And Joshua set up at Gilgal the twelve stones they had taken out of the Jordan."
(Joshua 4:20)

My Precious Child,

Did you know that I have great plans for those I love? In fact, Scripture proves repeatedly that the children of Israel did great exploits, when they put their trust in Me. The Book of Joshua details many scenes where they wanted to remember momentous events, so they erected great piles of massive stones to mark the occasion. Then, any time someone passed that way, the stories were repeated, passed down from one generation to another of My faithfulness from times past. The most memorable of these events was the conquest of the Promised Land, against all odds. The giants were many and fierce, yet the children of Israel trusted Me to help them defeat their enemies. The same is true of you. Your giants can be many and fierce, yet you too have a God who is always there, not only beside you, but within you, in the Person of the Holy Spirit, to guide you and make a way where there is no other way to victory.

What are some of the momentous victories your God has won for you? Do you write them down and repeat those stories as a testimony to your children and your children's children? Do you share them with strangers, to build their faith in Me? Do you remind yourself of those victories when you need encouragement, not to give in when things look discouraging? David comforted himself with testimonies of My faithfulness in his past, in order to strengthen his faith for the future. You can do the same thing, keeping journals, or notes in your Bibles, to remind yourself of My great love and faithfulness toward those who are Mine.

Half of the battle is to keep your mind fixed on Me, and that becomes easier as you recount your blessings one by one, In fact, it's no coincidence that the land Joshua conquered was positively littered with stone memorials. Contagious faith goes hand in hand with meditating on Me and remembering all the amazing things I have done for you. Do it in remembrance of Me...

Unknowns

"He raiseth up the poor out of the dust, and lifteth up the beggar from the refuse, to set them among princes, and to make them inherit the throne of glory; for the pillars of the earth are the LORD›s, and He hath set the world upon them."
(1 Samuel 2:8)

My Precious Child,

I deeply love My creation, especially those created in My image. In fact, I often take unknowns who have nothing—the despised, the rejected, the ignored—and lift them from the dung heap, setting them among princes. From prisons to palaces, I lift them up, and bring others down. All power belongs to Me.

Didn›t I take young David, the simple shepherd boy, and make him a mighty king to rule a nation with justice? Didn›t I exalt Esther, taking her from an unknown to a queen, using her to save her entire nation from certain destruction? Didn›t I strategically move Joseph from prison to palace to save his family and the world from starvation?

I do it all the time, so trust Me with your life—your everything. Stop trying to exalt yourself, and let Me exalt and use you. For only then you will be in tune with My spirit, and move in accord with your destiny.

Big doors often swing on very small hinges, so don›t belittle your circumstances, rather think of them as stepping stones to greatness. Don›t look down upon yourself in shame, but look up to Me instead.

Perhaps right now you feel invisible, like no one sees you at all. But don›t despise small beginnings, because I will have My way in your life if you allow it and make you more than you could ever have dreamed...

He Leads Me Beside Still Waters

Those That Have Been Forgiven Much Love Much.

"If I could speak all the languages of earth and of angels, but didn't love others, I would only be a noisy gong or a clanging cymbal. ² If I had the gift of prophecy, and if I understood all of God's secret plans and possessed all knowledge, and if I had such faith that I could move mountains, but didn't love others, I would be nothing. ³ If I gave everything I have to the poor and even sacrificed my body, I could boast about it; but if I didn't love others, I would have gained nothing."
(1 Corinthians 13:1-3, NLT)

My Precious Child,

I hear the deafening shriek of a rusty gate when my children lack tender compassion for others. I am a God whose very identity is mercy and love, and My thoughts are never far from a wayward child who has wandered off. I long for them to return to my table to feast on My presence, and be united with Me forever.

I am a God who does not give up on a lost sheep. In fact, I will leave the ninety-nine just to seek one caught in the briar. I walk with my lost ones in the darkest of nights holding them close and carrying them back home. I count the hairs on their heads; I know their names; no one escapes my love.

'Who pardons all your iniquities, Who heals all your diseases; Who redeems your life from the pit, Who crowns you with loving kindness and compassion; Who satisfies your years with good things, So that your youth is renewed like the eagle?' (Psalms 103:3-5) It is I, the Lord your God, and my face is always turned toward you.

Even as I have loved you with love that never ends, I want My people to abound with love for others. Let it never be said that you are bankrupt of love, but let your love be renowned as a healing oil that overflows to touch the least of these—the broken and needy.

Look into My eyes, and recognize the reality of My endless river of mercy and compassion for all mankind. That truth should be crystal clear, as I gave My very life for you. I was bruised for you. My arms opened wide in love as they nailed Me to that terrible cross; I was crowned with thorns and mocked, stripped naked and humiliated so that all My children could have eternal life. Nothing can affect or diminish My perfect love, so be Jesus with skin on to others! Let Me shine through you—let my healing oil be poured out so that the weary and worn may see Me in you.

The one who has been forgiven much also loves much. Have I not forgiven all your sins? Then go and let Me woo others with that same tender compassion poured out through you. Let My passionate love burn in you for the lost and wounded, so they see that I am God and there is a place for them in My heart. For then will you live out your destiny, and the world will be turned upside down for My glory!

My Recovery Room

"They cause the naked to lodge without clothing, that they have no covering in the cold."
(Job 24:7)

My Precious Child,

May I share with you a burden that's heavy upon my heart? There are many of My children who are naked—stripped of their nobility. They wear nothing but the shame of calamity, and they wander from place to place seeking refuge, but find none.

The winds blow, the rain beats down upon them and the thunder pronounces their doom. Their eyes are vacant—their cold, distant stares see nothing but more of the heartache that brought them to this awful place of anguish. They have become injured in the fight, too weak to go on. Whether their tragedy was caused through any fault of their own, or inflicted by others, they still have no place to rest or recover. Who will restore these weak ones back to health and honor?

He Leads Me Beside Still Waters

There is a desperate need of a recovery room for my wounded warriors! A place of healing, salvation, and unconditional love. In this special place of refuge, restoration and healing occurs, freedom takes place, and ugly scars are transformed into baby soft skin by My power.

It grieves My heart so when these wounded ones are turned away from My churches with nowhere to get out of the cold. My heart is grieved that so many churches are preoccupied with their own agendas and vision that there is no one to care for or listen to the broken ones. They have become insulated and apathetic, so that they can no longer feel the pain and heartache of those who need them most. I'm calling the church to be as a spiritual intensive care unit where all My children can find refuge, specialized care and recovery. I will send my dying, broken and repentant into such a church!

I am infusing My compassion and mercy into the hearts of those who are open to receive all of My children, holy and unholy alike. You live in a desperate time, where intensive care is needed more than at any other time in history. And because Satan knows his time is short he is bombarding the earth with temptation and snares. He seduces My children with all forms of ungodly temptations, and when they fall he mocks them for their weakness. Many have been wounded in the fight, yet many fallen warriors are desperate to come home and find healing and freedom. My deepest desire is to usher them in and equip them to stand as mighty warriors and defeat the enemy on our home court. I have already won this battle, but I need you to stand with Me, to bring it about in the natural. (See Exodus 14:4)

For those who have fallen into the depths of sin or suffering, we must provide a safe place of refuge, a spiritual care unit. So don't harden your hearts, or fail to show true compassion and mercy to those who repent and seek restoration and to be refreshed. I am the Great Physician, and it is I who performs the spiritual surgery. Your job is to gently nurse them back to health by leading them in prayers of repentance before God, after which they will see a mighty display of My power. The awful sting of death and the curse will be shattered, exchanged for life everlasting. The sin and malignancy that plague the soul will fall away, and healing will occur by My blood.

When desperate, fallen warriors are in the recovery room, they are not to be left alone. Never abandon them to heal on their own, rather embrace them, filling them with hope and encouragement from My Word, reassuring them that you will not leave them until they have fully recovered.

When I spoke of the ministry of the church, to feed the hungry and visit those in prison, I mentioned clothing the naked. (Matt. 25:36) If I place that much emphasis on physical needs, how much more should we clothe and minister to those whose spirits have been shamefully exposed? Tenderly clothe the wounded with love, peace and joy in the Holy Ghost; enfold the naked in a blanket of God's tender care, and keep them warm under a comforter of forgiveness and support.

These desperate ones are in My heart right now; they need "spiritual medics" filled with compassion to come to them with words of healing and hope. They need gentle, intensive ministry. In the Old Testament there were whole cities, called 'cities of refuge' where the needy could go to recover. Let my church be a city of refuge where recovery, healing, and restoration take place, nurturing back to health every wounded warrior regardless of how his wounds came about.

I have called the church to be a Bethesda—a place where the hurting can come and find healing; a place where the worst of the worst can receive mercy and forgiveness. When you, as My people, feed the hungry, heal the wounded, and love the lost, you are doing My will. So step out and let Me use you now!

"1-2 O my soul, bless GOD**.**

From head to toe, I'll bless his holy name!

O my soul, bless GOD**,**

don't forget a single blessing!

3-5 He forgives your sins—every one.

He heals your diseases—every one.

He redeems you from hell—saves your life!

He crowns you with love and mercy—a para-

dise crown.

He wraps you in goodness—beauty eternal.

He renews your youth—you're always young in his presence.»

(Psalm 103:2-5, MSG)

Unknotting of Knots

"Forasmuch as an excellent spirit, and knowledge, and understanding interpreting of dreams, and showing of hard sentences, and dissolving of doubts, were found in the same Daniel."
(Daniel 5:12)

My Precious Child,

Scripture tells us that Daniel had a ministry of shattering doubts. This fact was recorded in Aramaic, which is literally translated, "Daniel had the dissolving of knots." What a ministry he had! How many people do you know who are knotted up inside and can find no solutions to their problems? The stress of their struggles robs them not only of sleep but also of peace and joy. This burdens Me deeply.

Oh, My children, these same people walk through life crying out, "Oh God, let someone say something that will minister to me!" When the winds and storms of life blow, they don't know which way to turn. They bounce from pillar to post in confusion, desperate to know My will. I want you to know that in this day I'm raising up those who are so close to My heart that they will be able to deliver a word in season, a word that will untangle the knots, allowing these precious lambs to say to Me, "Thank you, Jesus. Now I see."

Daniel had an incredible ability to untangle knots—to interpret for Me. What's needed in the earth today is not just another moving oratory, but a voice who can interpret My heart to those who seek My face. And while hearts are touched by many wonderful sermons, most have done little to transform the inner man. On the other hand, the "voice of one crying" in the wilderness is so much in unity with the Father that transformation cannot be stopped, because the Holy Spirit does the work.

And while there is a great need for interpreters in your day, they are rare—one in a 1000.

'If there be a messenger with him, an interpreter, one among a thousand, to show unto man his uprightness.' (Job 33:23)

My children, I am searching for those who will carry My words—My vision—in their hearts. With holy fire on their lips they will speak My heart to a spiritually-famished generation. These dear ones are desperate for someone to untie their knots, for a revelation of the manifest presence of the living God. They are crying to hear My heart.

In the last days, there will be some who will prefer to speak from their intellect rather than to "wait on Me" for *"divine bread"* from heaven. It's far easier to speak from the mind or from a book than to seek earnestly for fresh manna to feed the hungry. That is not to say that you can't learn from others, but when messages to others lack substance and anointing because you did not seek *Me* first, I am grieved and you are shortchanged, settling for less than the true meat of the Word. I desire to fill your mouth with messages from My heart—words that will minister to wounded warriors with the thoughts from My heart especially for that particular moment in time. A current word for the right person, at the right time, in the right place is like apples of silver in frames of gold! And when you cease to share My heart your words are empty and heartless.

And because time is short, I'm raising up a voice on the battlefield, like the "voice of one crying in the wilderness," who will communicate My heart with a powerful prophetic anointing.

In these last days the true church will face its challenges, but it will not falter or fail. This new company of John the Baptists will prepare the way, carrying My heart just in the nick of time to a lost and dying world. They will love Me and refuse to water down the message. They will no longer compromise, nor will they rewrite the anointed Word of God to tickle the ears of listeners. Those with this anointing will never stifle the mighty movement of the Spirit.

Intellectual pursuits undertaken with man's wisdom are never an effective substitute for My transforming power. *I desire that you carry a living message to the battlefield, a* revelation, a communication from Me, to be passed on to My people at the prescribed moment. In fact, I'm looking for anointed vessels to open the heavens with the *"Word of the Lord,"* and not just to open an encyclopedia before My people. It's essential that I have vessels who know what it is to experience an open heaven, a personal encounter, and a personal revelation of Me.

I Will Restore You

"Come let us return to the Lord! He has torn us in pieces; now he will heal us. He has injured us; now he will bandage our wounds. In a short time, he will restore us so we can live in his presence."
(Hosea 6:1-2)

My Precious Child,

I say once more that I am a God of Restoration! You will recover all, and I will bring you back to life. Return to Me—humble yourself under My mighty hand, and I will raise you up again.

Consider this: A master builder walks through a deserted, dilapidated building, its walls bowed after years of neglect. Daylight filters in through holes in its rickety roof. The floors are soft and broken, creaking underfoot, weathered by years of cold and heat. Has this building suffered too cruel a fate to survive?

A nearby passer shouts, "All is lost—knock it down!' yet the Master builder does not see the deterioration, rather

He sees a vision of the stunning finished masterpiece.

Consider this, too: A master craftsman runs his hands over an old table, clearly deteriorated after years outdoors. The stain has long faded away, the nails rusted, the wood warped and worn.

A nearby passerby shouts, "All is lost—take it to the dump!" yet the Master hears not a word as he envisions the beautiful piece refinished and restored.

Finally, remember My prophet Nehemiah and the condition of My city, Jerusalem. Its gates had been burned; its walls were heaps of rubble. The once prosperous city lay in shambles. Nehemiah was heartbroken and went into mourning when he heard the awful news. But it was not My desire that Jerusalem lay in ruins, so I gave him a vision to rebuild!

Nehemiah 6:15 tells us that the repairs were completed in a record fifty-two days! Verse 16 says that all the surrounding nations cowered in fear as they watched it happen. In time, all of Jerusalem was restored!

My Precious One, I am that Master Builder, and I will restore you! You may feel weak and broken because of neglect of your spirit man. Perhaps you feel that your character has leaks and holes and your cherished name has been tarnished. I will restore you in the same way that the rickety, old table was restored to better than new.

Others may say, "All is lost—take it to the dump," but I say that I will heal you and bandage your wounds. I will rebuild you as I did Jerusalem, and others will see that I am your GOD! You are not worthless! All is not lost! Return to Me with all your heart. Humble yourself in My presence, and I will make all things new!

Steve Porter

Let My Kingdom Come!

"Let us celebrate, let us rejoice,
let us give him the glory!
The Marriage of the Lamb has come;
his Wife has made herself ready.
She was given a bridal gown
of bright and shining linen.
The linen is the righteousness of the saints.

The Angel said to me, "Write this: 'Blessed are those invited to the Wedding Supper of the Lamb.'" He added, "These are the true words of God!"
(Revelation 19:7-9, MSG)

My Precious Child,

I want nothing more than for you to draw near to Me to accomplish the *"end-time"* kingdom purposes for which I have drawn you to Myself. We're living in the last days! Prepare and make yourself ready!

Right now I'm equipping a body of 'overcomers' made ready through preparation. Much like a bride prepares for her wedding day, My bride will be prepared and ready, her lamp filled with oil, her life set apart to do My will. She is made ready and can testify that our Lord has "made us ... kings and priests," and as a result will have an active part with Me in the outworking of My end-time purposes to establish My Kingdom.

'Thy kingdom come. Thy will be done in earth, as *it is* in heaven.' (Matthew 6:10)

As My kingdom comes, chains are broken, lives are set free by My power, and people are delivered from bondage. When My kingdom comes mountains have to move; the earth shakes with the very manifest glory of God and every tongue declares that I am Lord. When My kingdom comes everything changes, creative power is released, darkness is defeated, and My bride will take her rightful place, where she will rule and reign with Me as My glory is made manifest through her. Others will take notice that she has been with Me, because she is beautiful and reflects My glory—My delight.

Today I stand at the door of your heart, knocking, eager for you to enter that intimate relationship with Me, as My stunningly beautiful, mature bride. I am not coming for an immature bride but rather for a bride prepared through her righteous acts. A right response when I knock will lead you into an active, personal relationship with Me that will result in you having *a part* in the establishing of, and functioning in, My Kingdom. This requires of you that you have a fixed upward gaze focused on Me, living a life surrendered to My will.

I am preparing a people in this day, who are being *made ready* to function in this higher realm of spiritual authority, which will affect both the church and the nations. Therefore, it is imperative that you spend quality time 'waiting' in the presence of the Lord with an upward gaze—that you might be able to hear and rightly respond to His call to function in His Kingdom as His mature bride. At this present time, there are those who are being called to "come up" into that higher level of relationship with Me. Will you answer the call, mighty warrior?

Dear Reader

If your life was touched while reading *He Leads Me Beside Still Waters* please let us know! We would love to celebrate with you! Please visit our website, www.findrefuge.tv

Consumed by His Presence,

Steve & Diane Porter

Steve Porter

Streams in the Desert.

In the barren wilderness where all seems forgotten
Runs a stream of life flowing from the only begotten

"Deep calls unto deep" with rivers flowing from his heart
My spirit is filled with the fullness when I come apart

Even when I feel dry and out of touch
I pray for His water that satisfies me much

There is a table in the wilderness, a place set for you
Come and dine at the Master's table, and drink and renew

His water is everlasting and never runs out
Refreshment from His glory like a waterspout

Come to the river that flows from His throne
Drink in the spirit deeply and know you're not alone

So next time you walk through that desert place
Take a drink from the fountain with His sovereign grace

—Steve Porter

He Leads Me Beside Still Waters

Here Comes My Beloved.

Here comes my Beloved; I see Him in the distance
His train fills the temple with glorious brilliance

I see Him standing there
Waiting for my love
Holding out His hand
Calling me His dove

His face is like no other
No words could ever express
When I heard Him speak to me
I could never second guess

He had the nurture of a Mother, the wisdom of a Father
Words that caused change, not babblings that would falter

"You're busy, doing all the time," said He
"Can you really hear Me, can you really see?
Your ears and eyes are closed, no longer do you hear
My heart you proclaimed that you held so dear

Steve Porter

"I miss My time with you
When we're all alone
Just Me and you together
When you lay before My throne

"Come up dear one to new level in Me
I'm calling you to a greater degree of intimacy

"Give Me of thyself, O gentle child
Come unto Me, let us reconcile"

After I heard Him speak I know I must have cried;
He put His arms around me and pulled me to His side

Be my constant companion, lover and a friend
Embrace me each day, my Lord; I will not offend

To be a Mary not a Martha is what I long to be
Thank you for taking the time to help me plainly see

—Steve Porter

He Leads Me Beside Still Waters

More books by Steve Porter

Crocodile Meat- *New and Extended Version*

Crocodile Meat- *Student Version*

Whispers from the Throne Room- *Reflections on the Manifest Presence*

Limitless

Letters to the Wounded Warrior- *God's Loving Message of Healing and Restoration for the Church*

He Leads Me Beside Still Waters- *50 Love Letters of Healing and Restoration from our Lord*

Coming in 2015-2016

The Tongue of the Learned- *How To Walk In The Prophetic Anointing*

Honor Forward- *A Man's Guide to Restore Honor, Valor, and Virtue*

The Beauty of your Presence - *Coming Alive in the Secret Place*

Steve Porter

Chambers of the King- *Reflections on the Song of Solomon*

Come and Follow Me- *50 Love Letters for the New Believer from our Lord*

For more info see our website

www.findrefuge.tv

Contact Info

Refuge Ministries

P.O Box 381

Bloomfield, NY 14469

www.findrefuge.tv

Rescue. Restore. Revive